Detective Science

Other Titles of Interest by Jim Wiese

Roller Coaster Science

50 Wet, Wacky, Wild, Dizzy Experiments
about Things Kids Like Best

Rocket Science

50 Flying, Floating, Flipping, Spinning Gadgets
Kids Create Themselves

Detective Science

40 Crime-Solving, Case-Breaking, Crook-Catching Activities for Kids

Jim Wiese

Illustrations by Ed Shems

John Wiley & Sons, Inc.

New York • Chichester • Brisbane • Toronto • Singapore

Wiese, Jim
    Detective science : 40 crime-solving, case-breaking, crook-
catching activities for kids / Jim Wiese : illustrations by Ed
Shems.
      p. cm.
    Includes index.
    Summary: Shows how detectives and forensic experts use science to
do their jobs and presents experiments that explore the world of
forensic science and criminal investigation.
    ISBN 0-471-11980-6 (pbk. : alk. paper)
    1. Forensic sciences—Experiments—Juvenile literature.
2. Criminal investigation—Juvenile literature. 3. Creative
activities and seat work—Juvenile literature. [1. Forensic
sciences—Experiments. 2. Criminal investigation. 3. Experiments.]
I. Shems, Ed, ill. II. Title.
HV8073.8.W54 1996   95-32953
363.2'5—dc20

Printed in the United States of America
10 9 8

For Elizabeth,

whose wonder of the world

keeps me young

Acknowledgments

There are many people who gave valuable time to help me research police forensic procedures and develop activities that would let young people experience detective science. Dennis Thrift of the Royal Canadian Mounted Police Forensic Laboratory in Vancouver, Gail Anderson of Simon Fraser University's Forensic Entomology Laboratory, David Sweet of the University of British Columbia's Forensic Dentistry Laboratory, and Mark Skinner of Simon Fraser University's Department of Archaeology were key in the development of some activities. They also related stories showing how the procedures in *Detective Science* have been used in their own work and reviewed the materials to make sure that they were accurate. I would also like to thank Alan MacKinnon of Simon Fraser University's Faculty of Education for his ideas on forensic science and the many long talks we've had about how best to reach students. Thanks to them all.

Again my special thanks go to John Wiley & Sons, especially my editor, Kate Bradford, and her assistant editor, Kara Raezer, who helped transform the concept of *Detective Science* into a carefully crafted book.

Contents

Introduction

Everybody loves a good mystery. Mysteries can take us out of ourselves and lead us to explore the far reaches of our imaginations. But mysteries don't just happen in books, on TV, and in the movies. Unfortunately, crimes like robbery, kidnapping, and others happen in real life, too. A **crime** is any act that is against the law. We continually hear about crimes in the news. When we find out about a crime, we often wonder: "Who did it?" "How did it happen?" and "Do we have any proof?" You may be surprised to learn that science often provides the answers to these and other questions about crime.

Forensic science is the study of objects that relate to a crime. These objects are called **evidence**. Forensic scientists study evidence so that it can be used as proof in court. The term **forensic** means "suitable for a court of law."

When analyzing evidence, forensic scientists perform the same activities that all scientists do: They observe, classify, compare, use numbers, measure, predict, interpret data, and draw **inferences**, or reasonable conclusions based on evidence. Forensic science is active and restless. It leaves no stone unturned.

The World of Detectives and Forensic Scientists

Forensic scientists can be police officers or **detectives**, special police officers responsible for investigating serious crimes. They can also be members of a city, regional, or state forensic laboratory and work along with detectives and the police. Some forensic scientists have a general background in **criminology**, the study of crime. Others specialize in the area of **pathology** (the study of the causes of death and disease), chemistry, biology, dentistry, psychiatry, psychology, or engineering.

Large police departments and national crime-fighting organizations, such as the Federal Bureau of Investigation (FBI), have their own forensic scientists. In smaller police departments, the police officers often serve as both forensic scientists and investigators. Many states have regional forensic laboratories that work with all local police departments. There are about 400 forensic laboratories in the United States, and about 40,000 forensic scientists and technicians. Most forensic scientists have university degrees in either criminology or a specialized field. A forensic scientist may also work in a university's biology, chemistry, anthropology, or criminology department, and be called in to work with the police department or local forensic laboratory when needed.

At the scene of a typical crime, a detective takes notes, interviews witnesses, and sometimes collects evidence. Forensic scientists may also collect evidence. The evidence is then sent to the **forensic laboratory**, also called the **crime lab**, to be analyzed. The forensic scientists at the laboratory use their skills in classification, comparison, observation, and reconstruction to examine the evidence. They sometimes work "blind," meaning they don't know other details about the crime. The results of their work reveal more about the crime and are given back to the detective. This evidence is added to the information gathered from the interviews. The detective, working with the forensic scientists, is then responsible for making an inference based on the evidence and solving the crime.

How to Use This Book

This book is full of information and simple experiments that will show you how detectives and forensic scientists use science to do their jobs. The book is divided into chapters based on general topic areas. Each chapter contains many exciting projects and experiments, and every project has a list of readily available materials you'll need and a step-by-step procedure to follow. Explanations are given at the end of each project. Some of the projects have a section called More Fun Stuff to Do, which lets you try different variations on the original activity. Another section, called Detective Science in Action, shows you how the scientific principles you learned doing the activity have been used to solve real-life crimes. Words in **bold** type are defined in the glossary at the back of the book.

You'll be able to find most of the equipment you need for the experiments around the house and at your neighborhood hardware, pharmacy, electronics, or grocery store. You don't need expensive equipment to be a good detective or forensic scientist. You need only to have an open mind that asks questions and looks for answers. After all, the basis of any good investigation is asking good questions and finding the best answers.

How to Do the Projects

■ Read through the instructions once completely and collect all the equipment you will need before starting the project or experiment.

■ Keep a notebook. Write down what you do in each project and what happens.

■ Follow the instructions carefully. *Do not attempt to do yourself any steps that require the help of an adult.*

■ If your project or experiment does not work properly the first time, try again or try doing it in a slightly different way. In real life, experiments don't always work out perfectly the first time.

A Word of Warning

Some science experiments can be dangerous. *Ask an adult to help you with experiments that call for adult help, especially those that involve matches, knives, or other dangerous instruments.* Don't forget to ask an adult's permission to use household items, and put away your equipment and clean up your work area when you have finished. Good scientists are careful and avoid accidents. Remember, real-life detective work can be hazardous. Do these activities only with friends, and in safe locations.

Elementary, My Dear Watson

Using Observation and Creative Thinking to Investigate Crimes

The power of observation is the best tool that a detective and a forensic scientist have. To **observe** is to note carefully, paying attention to details. When a detective collects data at a crime scene, observations are very important. Observations include everything from the objects found at the scene of the crime and statements from witnesses, to the time of day the crime took place and the temperature of the room where it occurred. A detective looks for **clues**, which are real, measurable, countable observations of the crime and the crime scene.

A detective does not know what data or evidence will eventually prove to be important, so he or she observes everything. At the scene of the crime, the detective and forensic scientist work together to make sure that all possible evidence is collected for later examination. If the evidence is badly handled, wrongly labeled, or allowed to become contaminated, it will be useless in the laboratory and the courts. Worse, if clues are overlooked, the detective will get no second chance.

In addition to making observations and gathering clues, a detective conducts interviews. He or she may also **tail,** or secretly follow, a person the detective thinks could be guilty of a crime, called a **suspect.** The detective uses this information, along with the evidence from the crime lab, to form a **hypothesis**, or an educated guess, about how the crime was committed and who did it. Detectives, like scientists, always keep an open mind during an investigation and look for hypotheses that could explain the crime.

PROJECT 1
You're the Detective

Your mother picks you up from school one afternoon. Before returning home, she has to stop at the bank to make a deposit. The two of you stand in line at the bank, waiting for your mother to be helped. Suddenly, one of the tellers screams, "We've been robbed!" What did you see while you were standing in line that might help with the investigation of the crime? Use your powers of observation to see what you remember.

Materials

picture on the next page   pen or pencil
timer   paper

Procedure

1. Observe the picture on the next page for exactly 30 seconds. Look at everything that you think might be important.

2. After 30 seconds, cover the picture and answer the questions below. Write the answers on the sheet of paper.

3. How observant were you? Compare your answers to the picture.

Questions

1. What time was it on the clock?

2. What was the date?

3. Describe the person at the front of the line. Was it a man or a woman? Was he or she wearing a hat? What kind of clothes was the person wearing? Could you tell how tall the person was? Did he or she have any distinguishing features?

4. Did you notice anything unusual in the picture?

More Fun Stuff to Do

Repeat the activity, but this time put the picture away overnight and try to answer the questions the next day. How good is your memory of the picture after 24 hours?

Explanation

When you observe, you create in your mind images of what you see. But what you see also has to be transmitted to your brain and stored in order for you to remember it later. As you found out in this activity, there is a lot of room for error in this process. When you first observed the picture, maybe you didn't notice certain details. Or maybe you saw details but didn't think they were important enough to make a point of remembering them.

If you did the More Fun Stuff to Do activity, you also know that time affects memory. Much of what we observe is stored in our **short-term memory**, and we remember it only for a few hours, or maybe only a few minutes.

If we store observations in our **long-term memory**, however, we may remember them for years. Repeating something over and over helps us remember it. Another helpful way to remember something is to associate it in our minds with something else. For example, most people would not be able to draw a map of Poland from memory. But if asked to draw a map of Italy, many people would be able to draw a fairly good sketch. Why? Because the shape of Italy resembles a boot. The shape of Italy sticks in our mind because we associate it with a common shape.

You can improve your powers of observation by doing the following exercise. Look at a department store display window for 30 seconds, then turn away and write down everything that you saw. Compare your notes with the real thing and write down the items that you left out. If you keep practicing this, your powers of observation will greatly improve.

PROJECT 2
Mystery Box

Good observation skills involve all the **senses** (the ability of the brain and nerves to react to the world around us through sight, hearing, smell, touch, and taste). Sight is just one of the senses. What a forensic scientist, detective, or witness hears, smells, feels, or tastes may also be important clues. Try the following investigation to sharpen your nonvisual observation skills.

Materials

empty shoe box or similar box with lid

various objects made from different materials—such as a rubber ball, a roll of toilet paper, a metal jar lid, a bar of soap, a plastic toy, a piece of fruit such as an apple, banana, or orange, etc.—gathered by your helper without your knowledge

helper

Procedure

1. Leave the room.

2. Have your helper put several of the objects in the shoe box and put the lid in place.

3. Return to the room and, without opening the box, try to guess how many objects are in the box and what the objects are made of. If possible, guess what the objects are. You can tilt, gently shake, and smell the box to help you.

4. After you have made your predictions, open the box and see how well you did. What objects were the easiest to determine? What objects were the hardest to determine?

5. Repeat the activity with other objects. Give your helper a turn at guessing.

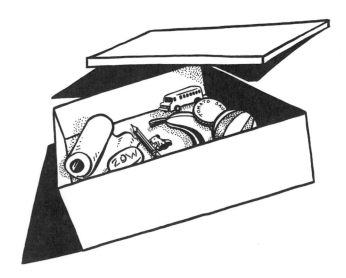

To develop your sense of touch, have a helper first blindfold you and then put several objects in front of you. Touch the objects, but do not pick them up. Can you identify them? Without removing the blindfold, pick up those that you could not identify. Can you tell what they are now? Remove the blindfold and see how well you did. Repeat the activity with other materials, but this time have your helper wear the blindfold.

Explanation

Forensic scientists and detectives must use all five of their senses when investigating a crime. They often use the sense of sight to observe the scene of the crime and record what they see. But often the other four senses—hearing, smell, touch, and taste—will give a forensic scientist information that may or may not be important evidence or clues. For example, the faint smell of bitter almond in a drinking glass might mean cyanide poisoning. Three loud bangs heard by witnesses could be gunfire or just a car misfiring.

Here is an exercise that you can use to improve your other senses. Sit on a park bench on a warm spring day. Close your eyes and observe what is happening around you. Can you identify five sounds that you hear? Can you identify three smells?

PROJECT 3
The Scene of the Crime

It's no exaggeration to say that following proper procedures during the first investigation of the crime scene can make the difference between a solved crime and an unsolved one. Try the following activity to learn some of the procedures performed at the scene of a crime.

Materials

your bedroom or another room of your house

several sheets of white paper

marking pen

masking tape

pen and/or pencil

notebook

camera (optional)

tape measure

several plastic bags

Procedure

1. Pretend a crime has been committed in the room you've selected. Suppose something has been stolen from the room.

2. Secure the scene of the crime. With a sheet of paper and the marking pen, make a sign that reads, POLICE INVESTIGATION. DO NOT ENTER. Use the masking tape to tape the sign across the entrance to the room.

3. Begin to record your observations of the room in your notebook. Remember, when investigating a crime scene, you cannot know what is important and what isn't. You need to record everything you find. If you have a camera, take several pictures of the room.

4. Use another sheet of paper and the pencil to make a sketch of the room. Measure the dimensions of the room using the tape measure, and record the measurements in the sketch. Draw in window and door locations and the placement of any furniture.

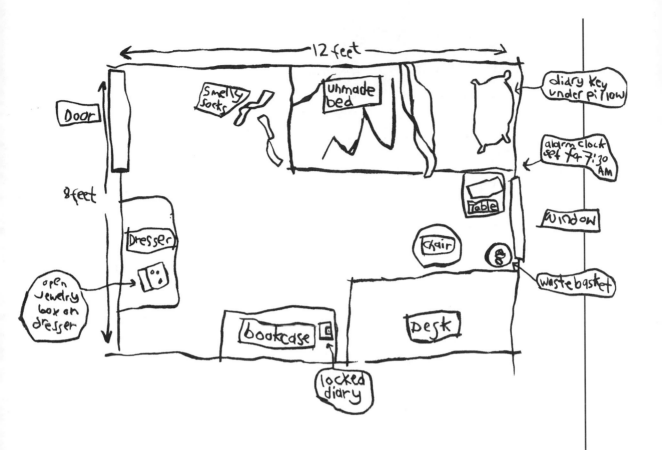

5. Examine the room carefully. Record your observations in your notebook. Add to your room diagram the location of any important items you find.

6. Begin to look for physical evidence. Physical evidence may include hair and fibers, a glass or other object that could contain fingerprints, a diary or notebook, or anything else you think might be important. Examine the waste basket. What do its contents tell you?

7. Save each piece of physical evidence in a plastic bag to examine later using the procedures you'll learn in this book.

The first duty at the crime scene is to secure the scene of the crime. This is usually done by the first police officer to arrive. If a person is badly injured at the scene, the officer will give assistance and call for medical aid.

Many crimes are investigated by the police officer on duty, but in more serious crimes, such as those that involve serious injury or the loss of expensive objects, a detective is often assigned to the case. A detective has usually received additional training, beyond that given to a police officer, in how to investigate a crime. When the detective arrives, he or she begins to record the scene of the crime by taking photographs, making sketches of the site, and taking notes.

The detective or members of a special forensic science team collect physical evidence. Physical evidence collected from the scene of the crime is stored in labeled bags or containers, and then sent to the forensic science laboratory for later investigation.

The investigators at the crime scene must be very careful to collect and preserve all physical evidence and to record all of their observations. These data will be used later to solve the crime.

Detective Science *in Action*

You never know when something unusual found at the scene of a crime will be important to an investigation. In 1994 Dr. Gail Anderson, a forensic **entomologist** (a scientist who studies insects), was asked to aid wildlife enforcement officials who were trying to put a stop to **poaching** (the killing of wildlife either without a license or out of season). In British Columbia, Canada, poachers often kill black bears and take their gallbladders, small internal organs that are valuable in certain cultures.

Investigators found insects on several black bears that had been killed by poachers. Dr. Anderson knew that insects have specific stages of development, from egg to adult. By examining the stage of the insects' development and working backward, she was able to approximate the actual date the bears were killed. Wildlife officials could then focus their investigation on individuals who were in the area on that day. The insects found on the bears eventually led to the arrest of the poachers.

PROJECT 4
Interviewing Witnesses

During an investigation, much of a detective's time is spent interviewing witnesses and questioning suspects. If everyone tells the same story, a detective can feel confident that he or she has learned the truth about a crime. But often people lie, or they believe they are telling the truth but are mistaken. Try the following activity to see how good you are at interviewing witnesses.

Materials

copy of the picture on the next page

watch or clock

pen or pencil

notebook

several helpers

Procedure

1. Have all of your helpers but one leave the room.

2. Give a copy of the picture on the next page to the helper.

3. Using the watch or clock, give your helper 1 minute to look at the picture, then take the picture away.

4. Ask your helper what he or she remembers about the picture. Ask questions like "How many people were in the picture?" or "Was there anything unusual that you noticed?" Record the answers in your notebook.

5. Repeat the procedure with each of the remaining helpers, making sure that the helpers do not hear each other's answers to your questions.

6. Compare the comments that the helpers made. How many details were mentioned? Did some statements conflict with other statements?

More Fun Stuff to Do

Stage a pretend crime during a party or family gathering, and see whether any of the guests can figure out who did it. You could have someone "steal" some books off a shelf or remove a candlestick. At some point after the crime, choose several guests as witnesses and question each in a separate interview. How did their observations compare? Were their observations good enough for them to figure out who took the books?

Explanation

When interviewing witnesses to a crime, there are several questions that detectives ask to get a description of and information about the suspect. Some typical questions include: What is the sex, race, and approximate age of the suspect? What is his or her height, weight, color of hair and eyes, and complexion? Did you notice any physical scars or marks? Did the suspect wear glasses or have facial hair? What was the voice like? What was the suspect wearing? What did the suspect do?

Interviewers must listen for unexpected information. Often the questions will cause the person who is being interviewed to **implicate** another person, meaning the person will reveal, by accident or on purpose, that someone else was involved in the crime.

Interviewers should remain impartial when they interview witnesses. This means they should not reveal their own opinions or feelings during the interview. Also they must be careful not to lead a witness to say something that is not true.

Interviewing witnesses and other methods of crime detection are similar to scientific investigation in general. Scientists bring their own thoughts and opinions to their experiments. Often they want an experiment to turn out a particular way, so it is difficult for them to remain impartial. This explains why two scientists, seeing the same information, can come to two opposite conclusions. Each bends the information to support his or her own views. Whether investigating crimes or performing experiments, scientists must always keep an open mind and be ready for unexpected data.

PROJECT 5
Tailing a Suspect

Sometimes during an investigation, a detective has to tail, or follow, a suspect. The suspect may make contact with other suspects or might lead the detective to more evidence. Try the following activity at school or another safe location to test your ability to tail a person.

Materials

notebook

pen or pencil

watch

several helpers

Procedure

1. Gather several helpers together. Inform them that at some point during the next week, you are going to tail one of them as part of an experiment. (Telling them that you are going to tail them makes your task more difficult but will avoid their embarrassment.)

   CAUTION: Tail the person at school or in another safe location, such as a party. Never wander around alone.

2. Choose a day and select one person to follow for one hour. Use your notebook to record notes of his or her activities and any people the person encounters. Record the time for all notes you make.

3. When you have finished tailing the person, review your notes. Are there any activities that surprised you? Could you tell exactly what happened during each encounter with other people? Did the person figure out that you were tailing him or her?

Detectives seldom follow a suspect by themselves. They usually work in teams to prevent the suspect from getting suspicious. Often a second, third, or even a fourth detective will pick up the trail where the previous detective leaves off. Try using a team to trail one of your helpers.

It is difficult to tail a person without being noticed. If a suspect sees the same person, especially a stranger, over and over again, the suspect's brain is alerted that something out of the ordinary has happened. He or she will become more cautious and will try to see whether someone is indeed tailing him or her. This is why the police use teams to follow suspects. One person will follow the suspect for a short time, then a second, third, or even a fourth detective will pick up the trail. The suspect does not see the same person, so the suspect's brain is not alerted that something unusual is happening.

Tailing a suspect is a form of surveillance. The term **surveillance** comes from the French word *surveiller*, which means "to watch over." Police practice surveillance for many reasons. They may watch a suspect's home or place of work in order to gain information or even to catch the suspect. This is sometimes called a **stakeout**. They may tail a suspect to get other information, such as a suspect's habits, daily routine, personal contacts, place of work, home address, or type of transportation used.

The detective can use the information gathered from observing a suspect to form a hypothesis or theory about the suspect, just as a scientist uses information to form a hypothesis about an experiment. For example, if a suspect meets with the same person at the same time every day and is seen passing slips of paper to that person, then the detective might make the hypothesis that the suspect is involved in a gambling operation and that the slips of paper are betting slips. The detective will then continue to investigate to determine whether that hypothesis is correct, in the same way that a scientist will test a hypothesis through experimentation.

Excuse Me, but Does This Belong to You?

Investigating What's Left at the Scene of a Crime

During the investigation of a crime, law enforcement officials collect evidence. This evidence, along with witness statements, is later used in courts to prove that a crime was committed and to convict the person or persons responsible for committing that crime. To **convict** means to find guilty, in a court of law, of committing a crime.

In 1910 at the University of Lyons, Edmond Locard first recognized the value of evidence to solve crimes and convict criminals. He developed a theory about evidence called the **contact trace theory**. This theory states that criminals will always take with them a trace of something from the scene of the crime, and will always leave behind some trace of having been there. The contact trace theory is the foundation of forensic science. The job of forensic science investigators is to locate the **trace evidence**, subject it to analysis and comparison in a forensic science laboratory, and then use all of the evidence to figure out what happened at the scene of the crime.

PROJECT 1
Lip Prints

Women who wear lipstick often leave lip prints on drinking glasses. At a crime scene, this kind of print would be collected as evidence during an investigation. Try the following activity to learn how lip prints can be used to solve crimes.

Materials

lipstick
   (dark colors work best)

white paper

pen or pencil

1. Put lipstick on both of your lips. Rub your lips together to spread the lipstick evenly.

2. Fold the white paper in half.

3. Place the folded piece of paper between your lips and firmly press your lips against it. Be careful not to slide your lips on the paper or else the lip print will smudge.

4. Remove the paper and unfold it. Write your name on the paper to identify the lip print as yours.

5. Examine your lip print. What do you notice about it? Are there any unique qualities that would let you identify it as yours?

Collect lip prints from several helpers. Make sure that you write each person's name next to his or her print. Then leave the room and have one of your helpers make a lip print on a drinking glass. Can you identify who made the print?

More Fun Stuff to Do

Explanation

There are many ways to identify a person. One of them is **cheiloscopy**, or the study of lip prints. (The term *cheiloscopy* comes from the Greek word *cheilos*, meaning "lip.") Lip prints are unique and do not change during a person's life. Although they are less commonly encountered than fingerprints at the scene of a crime, lip prints found on drinking glasses, cups, and even letters can be valuable evidence. One problem with lip prints is that their credibility has not yet been established in courts of law.

Lip prints are commonly classified into eight patterns. The five most common patterns are shown here.

**COMMON
LIP PRINT
PATTERNS**

diamond grooves

branching grooves

rectangular grooves

short vertical grooves

long vertical grooves

D etective Science *in Action*

Criminals are often caught because of the mistakes they make. A robber in Vancouver, Canada, was preparing to enter a bank for a holdup. He had his gun in one hand and a gym bag to hold the loot in the other. He didn't have a free hand to hold his note, which read, "This is a stickup. Give me all your cash." So he stuck the note in his mouth and held it between his lips. The robbery went off without a hitch, but the bank robber was later caught and convicted, in part because of the lip prints he left on the note.

P ROJECT 2
Taking Fingerprints

People have noticed the subtle differences in fingerprint patterns for hundreds of years. Centuries ago, Chinese and Japanese emperors signed papers with thumbprints to make them authentic. But it wasn't until the late 1800s that fingerprints were used as evidence to link a suspect to a crime. The first step in understanding fingerprints—and fingerprinting—is to examine your own.

Materials

magnifying lens
ink pad
several sheets of white paper
marking pen

pencil
transparent tape
helper

Procedure

1. Look at your fingertips through the magnifying lens and examine the patterns on your skin. These are your fingerprints. Can you describe them in words?

2. Make a set of your fingerprints. There are two easy ways to do this.

Method I

a. Press one finger at a time into the ink pad, being careful not to get your fingers too wet.

b. Have your helper make your fingerprints by holding your hand steady and pressing and rolling your

fingers one at a time onto a clean sheet of white paper. Be careful not to smudge the prints.

c. Use the marking pen to label each print with the name of the finger from which it came: thumb, index finger, middle finger, ring finger, pinkie.

Method 2

a. Rub the pencil point back and forth many times on a clean sheet of white paper to make a small dark area of pencil-lead dust.

b. Press one finger at a time into the dust. You may need to rub the pencil point again to get more dust for each fingerprint.

c. Have your helper place the sticky side of a piece of transparent tape on each dusted finger.

d. Tape the prints to another clean sheet of white paper.

e. Use the marking pen to label each print with the name of the finger from which it came.

3. Examine both types of fingerprints with a magnifying lens.

More Fun Stuff to Do

Using either method, create a complete set of fingerprints for each of several helpers. Use one sheet of paper for each set, and label the prints so that you know which fingers and which person they came from. Next, have each helper make a fingerprint on a separate sheet of paper. Do not label these prints. Choose one of the sheets of paper at random. Using your labeled sets of fingerprints, try to figure out whose fingerprint it is. What can you do to make the task easier?

2 Ask an adult to arrange a trip to your local police station to observe how the police take fingerprints. How do their methods compare to the two methods you learned?

Explanation

The skin on the palms of our hands (and the soles of our feet) is covered with tiny raised lines, called **friction ridges**. These ridges allow people to pick up and handle objects easily. Each person, even an identical twin, has a totally unique pattern of ridges on his or her hands and feet. And for each person, the pattern on each finger or toe is unique and different from the pattern on every other finger or toe.

A **fingerprint** is an impression of these ridge patterns transferred to a surface. Fingerprints occur because glands in our hands and feet secrete liquids, mainly sweat and oils. These liquids leave the patterned mark of our fingerprints on almost everything we touch.

There are three ways that fingerprints are valuable as evidence. First, fingerprints can confirm the identity of a person. When a criminal is taken into custody, it is a fairly simple task to take his or her fingerprints and cross-check them against other prints. This will prove who the criminal is and determine whether he or she has a criminal record or whether he or she is wanted by the police. Second, fingerprints can be used to compare a suspect in custody with fingerprints left at the scene of a crime. Third, forensic scientists can compare fingerprints left at the scene of a crime with those of a known criminal whose fingerprints are on record.

PROJECT 3
Classifying Fingerprints

As you've probably learned in the previous activity, it is difficult to identify fingerprints. They are rather small and contain a lot of detail. To simplify their identification process, forensic scientists use a classification system. Try the following activity and learn to classify fingerprints.

Materials

magnifying lens

several sets of fingerprints, your own and those of helpers (see Project 2, Taking Fingerprints, for two fingerprinting methods)

Procedure

1. Use the magnifying lens to observe several sets of fingerprints. Do you notice characteristics that any of them share? Can you group the prints into categories to make the identification process easier?
2. Look at the common fingerprint patterns in the diagram. Notice that the arch and the loop can have several forms and may bend to the right or to the left.
3. Try to match the fingerprints that you have collected to one of the common patterns.

Explanation

There are several ways to classify fingerprints. In this activity, you have tried one of the easiest ways. More complex classification systems break down the common fingerprint patterns into smaller groups. For example, forensic scientists divide arches into plain arches (arches that are rounded) and tented arches

COMMON FINGERPRINT PATTERNS

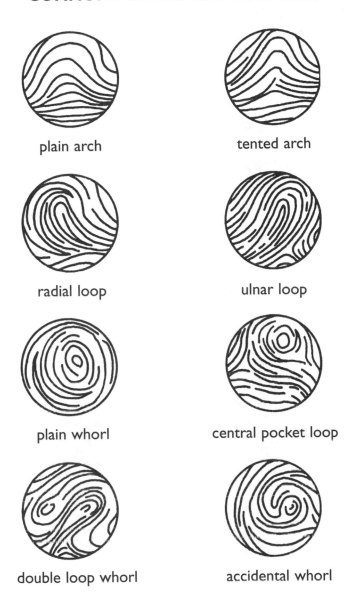

plain arch

tented arch

radial loop

ulnar loop

plain whorl

central pocket loop

double loop whorl

accidental whorl

(arches that are pointed). Loops can be either radial loops, which loop from the right, or ulnar loops, which loop from the left. Similarly, whorls are classed into several subdivisions.

Even more complex classification systems, such as the Henry System, have been developed to help compare fingerprints. The **Henry System** uses a number system to classify the characteristics of a fingerprint as well as the type of finger and hand from which it came. Investigators match a fingerprint to a person by matching the print's numbers to other prints with the same numbers, rather than by individually comparing a suspect's fingerprint to every fingerprint on file.

Fingerprints used to be examined and classified by hand. This was a slow, time-consuming process. Now computers can scan a fingerprint and compare it to huge files that have been collected from many police agencies, such as the FBI. This system, called **AFIS** (Automatic Fingerprint Identification System), can do the work in a fraction of the time. For example, it takes AFIS only two minutes to complete a fingerprint comparison that used to take years to complete by hand.

There is one limitation to AFIS and all fingerprint identification methods. Although there are over 250 million people in the United States, there are only about 10 million sets of fingerprints on file in AFIS. If a criminal's fingerprints are not on file, the system does not work.

PROJECT 4
Dusting for Fingerprints

How can detectives identify fingerprints left at the scene of a crime? They must remove the prints and transport them back to the crime lab, where they can compare them to other fingerprints on file. One way to locate fingerprints is by a technique called **dusting**. The fingerprints are coated with powder, then lifted and taken to the lab for identification. Try the following activity to learn how to dust and lift fingerprints.

Materials

drinking glass

cocoa

small paintbrush

transparent tape

5 sheets of light-colored
  construction paper

NOTE: You get a better fingerprint when more body oils are present. To do this, rub each finger alongside your nose or through your hair before making each fingerprint.

1. Press one finger at a time on the side of the drinking glass.

2. Sprinkle cocoa on the glass to coat the fingerprints.

3. Very gently brush the powdered area with the small paint-brush. When you've brushed off the loose powder, you should see the fingerprints.

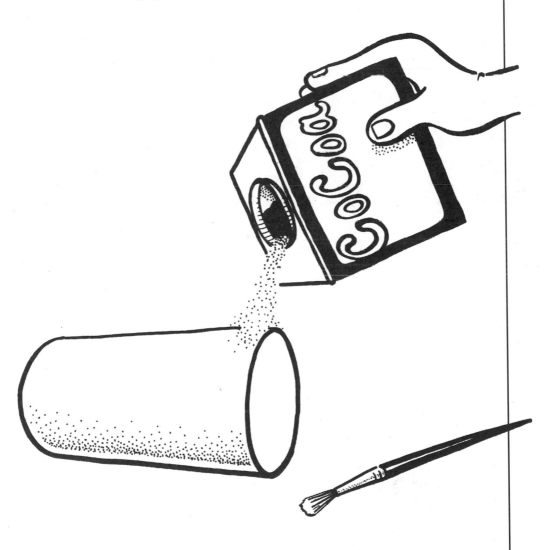

4. Lift each print from the glass by placing the sticky side of a piece of transparent tape on the dusted fingerprint and then carefully lifting the tape from the glass. The dusted fingerprint should stick to the tape.

5. Place each piece of tape on a separate sheet of light-colored construction paper.

More Fun Stuff to Do

Try to use other surfaces to dust for fingerprints. Put fingerprints on a variety of surfaces, such as wood, cardboard, aluminum foil, smooth paper, rough paper, cloth, glass, a plastic bag, and metal. Dust dark surfaces with talcum powder and light surfaces with cocoa. NOTE: Be careful to avoid breathing in the talcum powder, as it can irritate breathing passages. Place prints made with talcum powder on dark-colored construction paper and prints made with cocoa on light-colored construction paper. Which surfaces allow you to make fingerprints that can be identified using the dusting technique?

Explanation

If a criminal's hands are covered with dirt, paint, or other substances, his or her fingerprints may be easily seen. These are called **visible prints**. Other prints may be harder to see and may need treatment with chemicals or dust to make them visible. These are called **latent prints**. In this activity, you used dusting to make latent prints visible.

The best surface for dusting latent prints is one that is smooth, flat, and firm. Fingerprinting with powders does not work well on a surface that is rough or too flexible.

There are several powders that forensic scientists use to dust for latent fingerprints. Two common powders are (1) vegetable black, a fine carbon powder similar to the pencil scrapings that you used in Project 2, Taking Fingerprints, and the choice for light-colored surfaces, and (2) aluminum powder, a fine white powder used on dark-colored surfaces. Forensic scientists use a fingerprinting powder that contrasts with the color of the surface on which the fingerprint is located. This makes the dusted fingerprints more visible and easier to photograph for evidence.

Forensic scientists also add other chemicals, such as lead, cadmium, copper, and mercury, to fingerprint powders to make them stick better to latent fingerprints. Fluorescent and phosphorescent chemicals can also be added to fingerprint powder to make dusted fingerprints glow in the dark.

PROJECT 5
Tough Fingerprints

As you learned in Project 4, Dusting for Fingerprints, some surfaces are better than others for lifting fingerprints. On certain surfaces, even dusting will not make a latent print visible. However, forensic scientists have discovered new ways to make fingerprints visible on difficult surfaces. Try the following activity to learn how to collect tough fingerprints.

Materials

jar with a lid or other
   closable container
two 3-inch (7.5-cm) squares
   of aluminum foil

Super Glue (or any glue that
   contains cyanoacrylate)
timer

Procedure

1. Open the jar and set it on its side.

2. Put extra oil on your fingertip by rubbing it alongside your nose or in your hair.

3. Press the oiled fingertip on one square of aluminum foil, then put the foil in the jar.

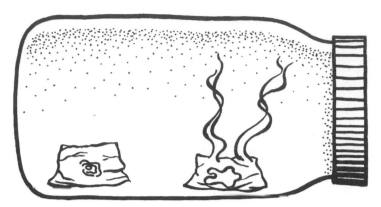

4. Squeeze a small amount of Super Glue onto the other foil square. Put the second piece of foil next to the foil in the jar.

CAUTION: Be careful not to get the glue on your hands.

5. Close the lid of the jar and wait about 30 minutes.

6. Observe the first piece of aluminum foil, the one your finger touched. What do you see?

More Fun Stuff to Do

Try this procedure with other materials. Repeat the experiment, substituting the aluminum foil with squares of cardboard, wood, cloth, and other materials that did not work very well in Project 4, Dusting for Fingerprints.

Explanation

A fingerprint made on aluminum foil cannot be detected using normal procedures, such as dusting, and has to be treated with chemicals. One such chemical is cyanoacrylate, a chemical used in Super Glue and similar products. In this activity, cyanoacrylate in the glue rises into the air. Trapped in the closed jar, this chemical sticks to the invisible oils in the fingerprint and hardens on them. As more and more cyanoacrylate particles harden on the fingerprint, it becomes visible and can then be easily identified.

There are other chemicals that can be used to make latent finger-prints visible on certain surfaces. Ninhydrin is a chemical that reacts with sweat and oils in the fingerprint to produce a purple image. It is ideal for lifting fingerprints from paper and some other porous surfaces, like bare wood and plaster. Iodine vapor can bring out fingerprints made on rough, absorbent, light-colored surfaces, such as paper and cloth. The iodine vapor reacts with the oil in the fingerprint and turns the fingerprint brown.

Detective Science *in Action*

Fingerprinting first played a major role in solving a murder in 1902. Joseph Reibel was found dead in his apartment in Paris, France. The detective assigned to the case was Alphonse Bertillon, one of the first detectives to collect and record the physical characteristics of criminals, including their fingerprints. At the crime scene, Bertillon found broken glass from a cabinet and blood on the carpet. It was obvious the intruder had cut himself and unknowingly left behind fingerprints on several pieces of the glass. By comparing the fingerprints on the glass to those of several known criminals, Bertillon was able to match them to the fingerprints on the record card of Henri-Léon Scheffer, a convicted swindler. Scheffer was picked up by the police, and burdened with guilt and remorse, he confessed to the crime.

PROJECT 6
Voiceprints

If investigators have a recording of a voice, they can use voice-prints, just as they use fingerprints, to help identify the person on the recording. A **voiceprint** is a pattern of wavy lines and whorls produced by a recording of a person's voice. Voiceprints are as unique as fingerprints. Try the following activity to sim-ulate your voiceprint.

Materials

glue

¼-by-¼-inch (6-by-6-mm) mirror

speaker with connecting wire (A speaker and connecting wire from an old radio is easiest to use.)

cassette recorder

wire cutters

flashlight

cassette recording of your voice

adult helper

NOTE: Ask an adult's permission to use the speaker.

Procedure

1. Glue the mirror to the speaker, about halfway between the center and the edge of the speaker.

2. Ask your adult helper to connect the speaker to the cassette recorder. This can usually be done by using wire cutters to remove ½ inch (1 cm) of insulation from the free end of the connecting wire and attaching the uninsulated wire to the speaker connection on the back of the cassette recorder.

3. Darken the room, then shine the flashlight onto the mirror. Note where the light reflects off the mirror and shines on the opposite wall.

4. Turn on the cassette recorder and play the tape. What happens to the light's reflection on the wall?

Explanation

Voiceprints can be used to identify a recorded voice. In this activity, the recorded voice creates vibrations that are sent to the speaker. These vibrations are unique to the voice and to the words that are being said. The vibrations cause the speaker and the mirror attached to it to move, which causes the light reflected off the mirror to move in the same direction. If you could mark the path that the reflected light traced, you would have a line that is similar to a voiceprint. It would be possible to identify who, or what, made the sound.

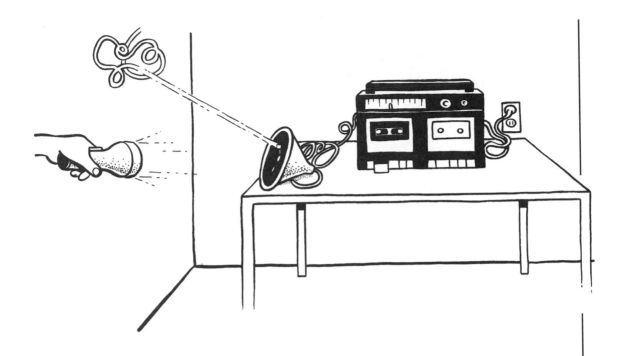

Forensic scientists use voiceprints to compare recorded voices. They normally have a suspect record a 2½-second speech that uses the ten most common words: *a*, *and*, *I*, *is*, *it*, *on*, *the*, *to*, *we*, and *you*. They then compare the voiceprint of the suspect to the recorded voiceprint used as evidence in a crime.

Detective Science *in Action*

The first application of voiceprints occurred in Connecticut, where a voiceprint was used to prove the *innocence* of a suspect. The suspect was a man accused of using a telephone to make threats to a family. The principal victim claimed that the suspect had made the calls, while the suspect protested his innocence. Investigators made tape recordings of both the phone calls and the suspect's voice. An analysis of the phone calls revealed that they had actually been made by two individuals disguising their voices. The suspect was released and the two guilty persons were arrested.

PROJECT 7
Hair Specimens

Hair left at a crime scene can be important evidence in a forensic investigation. A strand of hair can indicate the age, sex, and race of the person from which it came. Microscopic examination of hair found at a crime scene can confirm that a suspect was at the scene. Not all hair evidence has to be human hair; for example, cat hair found at the scene of a robbery may match the cat hair found on a suspect's coat. Try the following activity to see how hair is used as evidence in an investigation.

Materials

strands of hair from several people or animals

transparent tape

several sheets of white paper

marking pen

magnifying lens

microscope (optional)

pen or pencil

notebook

Procedure

1. Obtain strands of hair from several people. You can take some from their hairbrushes, or cut or pull, *with permission*, several hairs from each head. Include pet hairs in your investigation, if possible.

2. Tape each strand of hair to a sheet of white paper. With the marking pen, label the hair according to whose it is and how it was obtained.

3. Examine each hair with the magnifying lens and microscope, if available. Record your observations in your notebook.

Ask a helper to choose someone who already gave you a hair sample and obtain another strand of hair from that person. Using your labeled samples and magnifying lens or microscope, can you identify this person after comparing all samples?

Explanation

The first step in any laboratory examination of hair evidence is for the crime lab to determine whether it is human hair. This is done by first comparing the hair to known human samples. The next step is to note the features of the hair, such as its length, diameter, and color, including the distribution of color (hair may be lighter on one end) and any evidence of dyeing or bleaching.

Hair that has been pulled from the scalp—as opposed to hair that has been cut or broken off, or that has naturally fallen out—will often have tissue sticking to the **root** (the enlarged part of the strand of hair that grows below the surface of the skin). This tissue can be used to identify the owner of the hair through forensic techniques such as blood factor analysis and DNA testing (see Chapter 4, Project 4, DNA Testing).

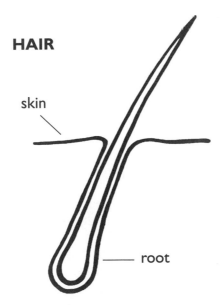

HAIR

skin

root

PROJECT 8
Cloth Fibers

Like hair, cloth fibers are among the most common items left as trace evidence at a crime scene. Forensic scientists analyze, identify, and compare cloth fibers to place a suspect at a crime scene. For example, wool thread caught on a window frame at a crime scene may match the sweater found at a suspect's house. Try the following activity to see how fibers can be used as evidence in an investigation.

Materials

several different fabrics, including some with natural fibers, such as cotton and wool, and some with synthetic fibers, such as nylon or rayon

transparent tape

several sheets of white paper

marking pen

magnifying lens

microscope (optional)

pen and pencils

notebook

NOTE: If you use old clothing, be sure to ask adult permission first, or ask at your local fabric store for fabric remnants.

Procedure

1. Pull fibers from several fabrics.

2. Tape each fiber to a separate sheet of white paper. With the marking pen, label the fiber according to which fabric it is from and how it was obtained.

3. Examine each fiber with the magnifying lens and microscope, if available. Record your observations in your notebook.

Ask a helper to pull a fiber from one of the fabrics without telling you which fabric it's from. Using your labeled samples and magnifying lens or microscope, can you identify what the fiber is and which fabric it came from?

Explanation

There are four sources of fibers: animal, vegetable, mineral, and synthetic. The most common animal fibers are wool, cashmere, and silk. The most common vegetable fiber is cotton. Asbestos is the only mineral fiber. Synthetic fibers make up about 75 percent of all textile fibers in the United States and are the most common fiber investigated in the crime lab. There are over 1,000 different types of synthetic fiber, classified by their chemical composition, fiber shape and size, additives, and manufacturing process.

Like hair, fibers are important trace evidence. A forensic scientist uses a vacuum cleaner to collect fibers, hairs, and dirt found at the scene of a crime. These materials are then taken to the crime lab to be analyzed and compared to known samples. Investigators can link a suspect to the scene of a crime by matching fibers found at the scene of a crime to fibers found on a suspect or in a suspect's vehicle or home.

PROJECT 9
Paper Fibers

A detective investigating a crime looks for any material that might connect a suspect with the crime scene. A burned match found in an ashtray can provide evidence that links a suspect to the crime. Try the following activity to see how the paper fibers of a torn match can help forensic scientists solve a crime.

Materials

3 identical unused
    matchbooks
magnifying lens

paper
pencil

Procedure

CAUTION: Do not light matches during this activity.

1. Tear one match out of each matchbook.

2. Use the magnifying lens to examine the torn end of each match.

3. Draw a sketch of the torn end of each match. Do you see any special features that would help you link the match to the matchbook from which it was torn?

4. Use the magnifying lens to examine each matchbook. Carefully examine where each match was removed from the matchbook. Can you find any evidence on the matchbook that would help you link the torn match to it?

While you are out of the room, have a helper remove a match from each matchbook. Can you link each match to the matchbook from which it was torn?

More Fun Stuff

Paper is made of various wood fibers that have been pressed together. These fibers are randomly arranged in the paper and can be of various lengths. When you tear paper, the fibers separate. Since no two pieces of paper have fibers that are identical in arrangement and length, all paper tears differently. Even if you tried, you could not make identical tears in two pieces of paper.

Matches in a matchbook are made of paper. The end of a paper match torn from a matchbook is distinctive and can be used to match it to the matchbook from which it was torn. If a match torn from a matchbook is found at a crime scene and can be linked to a matchbook found on a suspect, this evidence could prove that the suspect was at the scene of the crime.

PROJECT 10
Casts

Footprints, shoe prints, and tire tracks found at the scene of a crime can be important evidence to connect a suspect with a crime. A forensic scientist makes a **cast** (a form made by pouring plaster of paris into a mold) of this type of impression. Try the following activity and learn how to make a cast of a shoe print.

Materials

tape

2 pieces of 1-by-10-inch (2.5-by-25-cm) cardboard

2 pieces of 1-by-5-inch (2.5-by-12.5-cm) cardboard

petroleum jelly

shoes

soft soil in an outdoor area

plaster of paris

water

paper cup

craft stick

timer

newspaper

small paintbrush

NOTE: This is an outdoor activity.

1. Tape the four pieces of cardboard together to make a 5-by-10-inch (12.5-by-25-cm) rectangular frame. Grease the inside of the cardboard frame with petroleum jelly.

2. Wearing the shoes, press the sole of one show into soft soil so that you leave a shoe print in the soil.

3. Surround the shoe print with the cardboard frame.

4. Mix plaster of paris with water in the paper cup according to the instructions on the box of plaster. Stir with the craft stick.

   NOTE: Be sure to mix the plaster in a throwaway container. Do not pour plaster down the sink, as it can clog the drain.

5. Pour the liquid plaster over the print. Allow it to dry for 1 hour.

6. Lift the plaster cast out of the ground. The soil will stick to the plaster. Bring the plaster cast indoors and place it on newspaper. Allow the plaster to dry overnight.

7. Brush the loose soil from the cast with the paintbrush.

8. Observe the cast. What can you tell about the shoe that made the print?

Make shoe-print casts of several helpers. Can you identify which shoes made each print? Make a cast of the track made by a tire in mud. What can you tell about the tire by looking at the cast?

More Fun Stuff to Do

Explanation

Casts of impressions, such as shoe prints, tire prints, or even bare footprints, taken at the scene of a crime can connect a person or vehicle with the crime.

When a shoe makes an impression in soft material, such as soil, it leaves behind a negative mold of itself, including any special marks or imperfections. Signs of wear or a manufacturing detail, such as a logo or tread pattern, may be visible. By carefully filling the mold with the plaster of paris, investigators can make an exact reproduction of the surface of the sole of the shoe.

This reproduction is then sent to the crime lab where forensic scientists analyze it and compare it to known objects. For example, the pattern on the sole of a running shoe can be used to identify the brand of shoe, or the wear pattern may indicate that the wearer walks with a limp or drags one foot. Similar markings on a tire cast can tell forensic scientists what brand of tire made the mark, and may even tell what type of car the tires were on.

The soda machine at your school has been broken into and the money has been taken. Hall monitors stop two students from another school in the hallway and find a crowbar in one student's backpack. How can your school prove that these students committed the crime? Try the following activity to investigate how detectives can match tools to the scene of a crime.

Materials

hammer

16d nail (about 3 inches [7.5 cm] long)

scrap piece of plywood

pliers

crowbar

screwdriver

timer

adult helper

Procedure

NOTE: This activity requires adult help.

1. Have your adult helper use the hammer to pound the nail into the plywood so that ½ inch (1.25 cm) of the tip of the nail sticks out the back of the wood.

2. Leave the hammer, pliers, crowbar, and screwdriver near the plywood.

3. Tell your helper that he or she will have 3 minutes to remove the nail from the board, using several of the tools that are supplied.

4. Leave the room and time your helper for 3 minutes while he or she performs the task. *Do not watch while your helper removes the nail.*

5. When 3 minutes are up, try to match the marks made on the wood with the tools that were used. Which ones are easy to match? How could police use this information to investigate crimes?

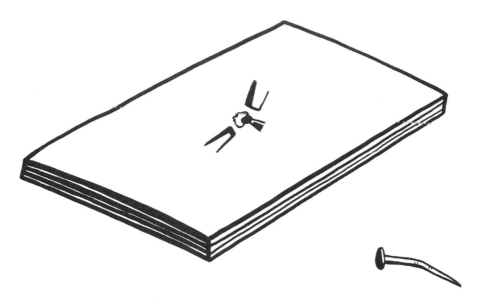

Explanation

Almost any device used to perform work can be called a tool, and almost every tool will leave behind some mark of its use. There are three categories of tool marks: *impressions*, such as those made by a hammer or a crowbar in a soft surface; *cut marks*, such as those made by wire cutters, saws, and the like on a material; and *scratch marks*, such as those made by a knife blade scraping over a surface. Like other forms of trace evidence, these marks can provide forensic scientists with clues about which tools were used at a crime scene. If the tools found on a suspect match the tool marks left at the scene of a crime, police have evidence to link the suspect to the crime.

One of the most frequently found tool impressions is the "jimmy" mark found at the site of a break-in or forced entry. These marks occur when a criminal wedges a jimmy—a crowbar, screwdriver, or tire iron—between a door and its jamb, or between a window and its sill, and exerts pressure until the door or window opens. The hard metal of the tool compresses the wood, leaving an impression of the tool in the wood.

PROJECT 12
Glass Fragments

Glass fragments are one of the most frequently found substances at crime scenes: Criminals break windows to gain entry into buildings, hit-and-run accidents result in broken glass, and so on. Try the following activity to see how forensic scientists analyze glass fragments at a crime lab.

Materials

jigsaw puzzle

CAUTION: Do not try this activity with actual glass fragments.

Procedure

1. Dump the jigsaw puzzle pieces onto a table or floor. Turn each piece facedown.

2. Assemble the puzzle using only the shape of the pieces as a clue, not the elements of the picture.

3. Did you find this easier or more difficult than usual?

Explanation

Forensic scientists at a crime lab use a technique called the **jigsaw method** to analyze glass fragments. The jigsaw method works because when glass breaks, its surface fractures unevenly. This breaking process produces unique shapes of glass that will lock only into the pieces that were next to them at the point when the glass broke, just as each piece of a jigsaw puzzle will lock only into the pieces that go next to it.

Forensic scientists use the jigsaw method of glass-fragment analysis to solve crimes. For example, investigators may want to know whether a piece of glass found in a hit-and-run victim's clothing matches the glass from a broken headlight of a suspect's automobile.

As you saw in this activity, the jigsaw method is very difficult. Forensic scientists perform other tests to match glass fragments to the scene of a crime.

PROJECT 13
Ballistics

A gun leaves an impression on the bullets that are shot from it. Forensic scientists can use these impressions to match bullets to the type of gun used. The field of science that studies bullets and other shot objects is called **ballistics**. Try the following activity to investigate how detectives can solve a crime by using their knowledge of ballistics to match bullets to a gun.

Materials

ballistic evidence shown in the drawing on next page

Procedure

1. Using the ballistic evidence shown, match the bullet found at the scene of a bank robbery with the sample bullets fired from several guns.

2. Which type of gun was used in the crime?

BULLET TAKEN FROM THE CRIME SCENE

BULLETS FROM GUNS IN EVIDENCE

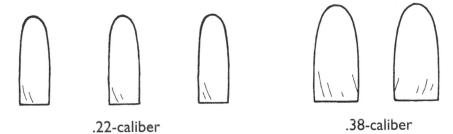

.22-caliber   .38-caliber

Explanation

The first thing that a forensic scientist will determine when examining a bullet is its caliber. A bullet's **caliber** is the same as its diameter, the length of a straight line through the center of the flat end of the bullet. The diameter of a bullet is measured in either inches or millimeters. A bullet that is 0.22 inches in diameter is a .22-caliber bullet. It is used in a .22-caliber rifle, which has a barrel 0.22 inches in diameter. Similarly, a 9-mm pistol uses a bullet that is 9 millimeters in diameter. Forensic scientists will compare the caliber of a bullet found at the scene of a crime to the caliber of a gun found on a suspect. But that is just the beginning of their ballistic analysis.

As early as the sixteenth century, gunsmiths were improving the speed and accuracy of guns by cutting grooves called **rifling grooves** around the insides of gun barrels. These grooves make the bullet spin down the barrel and in the air, thus increasing the speed and force of the bullet. Bullets are made slightly larger than the gun barrel to ensure a tight fit, which results in the characteristic **rifling marks** on the bullet after it has been fired.

Inside the gun barrel, the rifling grooves and the **lands** (the area inside the gun barrel that remains after the barrel has been grooved) create a distinctive pattern that does not change, so any bullet that passes through the barrel of a particular gun will bear the rifling marks of the gun. In addition to rifling marks made on the bullet, identifying marks are made on the **cartridge** (the cylindrical container of the bullet, which holds the gunpowder and stays in the gun when it is fired). These marks are caused by the **firing pin** (the piece of metal that strikes the cartridge and ignites the gunpowder).

Matching bullets to guns is one of the simplest procedures in forensic science. By knowing the caliber of a bullet and the land and groove configuration, a forensic scientist can tell detectives what type of gun the bullet came from.

INSIDE OF GUN BARREL

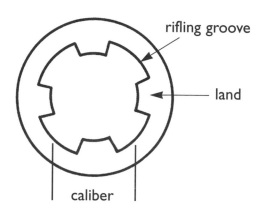

rifling groove

land

caliber

Detective Science *in Action*

Forensic evidence proves a person's innocence as often as it proves a person's guilt. Recently, for example, a prospector in Alaska was found in his remote cabin dead from a gunshot wound. The immediate suspect was the prospector's partner. Indeed, when the police found the partner, he was carrying a recently fired rifle and had blood on his boots.

A hundred years ago, the partner would have been found guilty based on those two bits of evidence alone. But forensic evidence showed that the bullet that killed the prospector came from a pistol, not the partner's rifle, and that the blood on the partner's boots came from a recently killed deer.

Mixing It Up

Using Chemistry to Analyze Evidence

The forensic science laboratory is a new idea in the United States and Canada. At the turn of the century, the FBI in Washington, D.C., began collecting a library of books on scientific subjects related to crime-testing blood, hair, and various drugs. But the St. Valentine's Day Massacre on February 19, 1929, was a turning point in the growth and development of a forensic laboratory. On that day, Al Capone's gang killed seven people in a Chicago garage. Police kept the bullets, hoping they could use them to identify the gun, but they had no crime lab. Two of the coroner's jurors investigating the crime heard of the police's plight and later helped finance a forensic laboratory in Chicago, the Northwestern University Crime Lab.

J. Edgar Hoover, head of the FBI, heard of Northwestern's lab and sent agents for a visit. They were so impressed that in 1932, the FBI started a forensic laboratory of their own. Today, the multimillion-dollar lab is the world's best-equipped scientific facility for criminal investigation.

The chemistry department is often the largest single unit in a forensic laboratory. Forensic scientists perform many tests that involve chemistry. **Chemistry** is the study of substances, including what they are made of, what they do, and how they react to other substances. Chemistry can be used for procedures such as matching the ink on a ransom note to a specific pen, identifying flammable liquids that may have been used in a case of **arson** (the criminal act of burning property such as a building), and testing different materials to see whether they are illegal drugs. Try the following activities to see other ways chemistry can help detectives solve crimes.

PROJECT 1
Mystery Powders

White powder found at a crime scene or in a suspect's pocket may be an illegal substance or merely sugar. A detective will have the crime lab identify the substance to determine whether a crime has been committed. Try the following activity to learn how forensic chemists use chemistry to identify unknown substances.

Materials

pencil
sheet of white paper
measuring spoon set
baking soda
sugar
salt
cornstarch
4 sheets of black construction paper

white chalk
magnifying lens
eyedropper
water
4 small jars
iodine solution (available at most drugstores)
dish towel
vinegar

Procedure

1. Use the pencil and white paper to create a chart similar to the one shown on the next page.

2. Put ¼ teaspoon (1 ml) of each white powder (baking soda, sugar, salt, and constarch) on a separate sheet of black construction paper. Use the chalk to label each powder.

3. Examine each powder with the magnifying lens. What does each powder look like? What is its shape? Are its grains large or small? Record your observations in the Appearance column of the chart.

	Appearance	Texture	Smell	Reaction to Water	Reaction to Iodine	Reaction to Vinegar
Baking Soda						
Sugar						
Salt						
Cornstarch						

4. Rub each powder between your fingers. How does it feel? Record your comments in the Texture column.

5. Do any of the powders have a smell? If so, record that information in the Smell column.

6. Use the eyedropper to place a drop of water on each powder. What happens? Do any of the powders dissolve or react in any other way? Record the results in the Reaction to Water column.

7. Put ½ teaspoon (2 ml) of each powder in a separate jar. Use the eyedropper to add 2 drops of iodine solution to each jar. Observe what happens and record your observations in the Reaction to Iodine column.

8. Rinse and dry the jars.

9. Put ½ teaspoon (2 ml) of each powder in a separate jar. Add 2 drops of vinegar to each jar. Observe and record the results in the Reaction to Vinegar column.

More Fun Stuff to Do

Can you identify a mystery powder? Have a helper give you a small amount of one of the white powders without telling you which one it is. Repeat the chemical tests on the mystery powder and compare your results to those on the chart to identify the powder. Check with your helper to see whether you were correct.

Explanation

The results of your tests in this activity should be similar to those listed in the chart on the next page.

If you did the More Fun Stuff to Do activity, you should have been able to identify the unknown substance by repeating the tests and comparing your results to the results listed in your chart.

Just as you did in this activity, forensic scientists use a variety of tests to identify an unknown substance. Some tests examine the physical characteristics of a substance, such as its color, shape, and so forth. Other tests explore how a substance behaves, such as whether it dissolves in water, how it reacts to an acid, and so on. Forensic scientists compare the results of tests done on unknown substances to the results of tests done on known substances to identify the unknown substances.

	Appearance	Texture	Smell	Reaction to Water	Reaction to Iodine	Reaction to Vinegar
Baking Soda	white, powdery, like fine sand	feels gritty	none	dissolves	no reaction	releases bubbles
Sugar	white, irregularly shaped crystals, some cube shaped	like sand	none	dissolves	no reaction	dissolves, but no reaction
Salt	white, uniform, cube-shaped crystals	like sand	none	dissolves	no reaction	dissolves, but no reaction
Cornstarch	white, fine powder	fine powder, sticks to fingers	none	makes white paste	immediately turns purple or black	dissolves, but no reaction

etective Science *in Action*

In New York Harbor, a cargo ship from Colombia was unloading boxes marked as ceramic pottery. Working on a tip, the Drug Enforcement Agency (DEA) raided the ship and opened the boxes. Bags of white powder were found inside several ceramic sculptures.

The first test done at the scene was the Scott test to determine whether the white powder was the illegal drug cocaine. Agents mixed a 2 percent solution of a chemical called cobalt thiocyanate with one part each of water and glycerin. When the white powder found in the sculptures was added to the solution, the solution immediately turned blue, establishing the identity of the white powder as cocaine. To confirm this identity, a concentration of another chemical, hydrochloric acid, was added to the solution, turning the blue-colored solution pink.

The ship and its cargo were held in the harbor so that a more thorough search could be undertaken. DEA officials eventually found over $50 million worth of cocaine on the ship. Both the importers of the ceramic pottery in New York and the exporters of the pottery in Colombia were arrested.

PROJECT 2
Mystery Substances

Any unknown substance found at a crime scene may be important evidence. The liquid left in a drinking glass might be a poison, or the residue found on a suspect's hand may be gunpowder. As you know, forensic chemists perform many tests on unknown substances in order to identify them. Color, odor, and reaction to other substances are all clues to the identity of an unknown substance. Try the following activity to perform another important test.

Materials

1½ quarts (1.5 liters) tap water

2-quart (2-liter) saucepan

2 red cabbage leaves

timer

colander

plastic bowl

marking pen

masking tape

5 jars or glasses

measuring cup

3 tablespoons (45 ml) concentrated lemon juice

3 tablespoons (45 ml) vinegar

3 tablespoons (45 ml) distilled water

1 tablespoon (15 ml) baking soda

3 tablespoons (45 ml) ammonia

pencil

sheet of white paper

adult helper

Procedure

NOTE: This activity requires adult help.

1. Put the water in the saucepan. Tear the red cabbage leaves into small pieces and place them in the water.

2. Have your adult helper heat the water to boiling and boil the leaves for 5 minutes. Allow the liquid to cool.

3. Hold the colander over the bowl and have your adult helper carefully strain the leaves through the colander. Throw the leaves away.

4. Use the marking pen and masking tape to label the jars from 1 to 5.

5. Pour about ½ cup (125 ml) of the cabbage juice into each jar.

6. Add the lemon juice to jar 1, the vinegar to jar 2, the distilled water to jar 3, the baking soda to jar 4, and the ammonia to jar 5.

   CAUTION: Be careful not to spill the ammonia on your hands.

7. Observe the color that each substance turns the cabbage juice, and record the color on a chart similar to the one shown.

Jar	Chemical	Acid/Basic	Color
1	lemon juice	acid	
2	vinegar	slightly acid	
3	distilled water	neutral	
4	baking soda	slightly basic	
5	ammonia	basic	

More Fun Stuff to Do

Use the remaining cabbage juice, ½ cup (125 ml) at a time, to test various household substances. Set up new jars of cabbage juice, add the substances to the juice, and observe the color the juice becomes. Based on the color, use your chart to determine whether the substance is acid, slightly acid, neutral, slightly basic, or basic.

Explanation

There are many tests that forensic scientists perform on unknown substances. A forensic scientist will first observe the unknown substance, gathering information about its physical characteristics, such as color, texture, odor, melting point, and boiling point.

Next, the forensic scientist will test the chemical characteristics of the unknown substance. Certain substances are chemicals called **acids** or **bases.** Cabbage juice is a chemical indicator that changes color in the presence of an acid or a base. If the substance tested is acid, the cabbage juice turns red. If the substance is basic, the juice turns green. Listed on the next page are the expected results for this activity.

Jar	Chemical	Acid/Basic	Color
1	lemon juice	acid	red
2	vinegar	slightly acid	pink
3	distilled water	neutral	dark purple
4	baking soda	slightly basic	light green
5	ammonia	basic	green

Litmus paper is another chemical indicator that can be used to test whether a substance is an acid or a base. You may have used litmus paper in school. The pH scale describes the strength of acids or bases. Sensitive pH paper or pH meters tell not only whether the unknown substance is acid or basic, but also how strong the acid or base is.

In addition to acid/base testing, further chemical tests are done by the forensic scientist to determine how the unknown substance reacts with other known substances. By matching these test results to the results of known substances, the forensic scientist can determine the identity of the unknown substance.

PROJECT 3
Blood Identification

A few drops of a red substance are found at the house of a missing person. Are the drops red paint, ketchup from a hot dog, or possibly blood? The identification of the substance is important and will help a detective know which way to direct an investigation. Try the following activity to see one way that investigators determine the identity of a red substance.

Materials

eyedropper

red watercolor paint

ketchup

blood (from the bottom tray of a meat container)

plate

tap water

Hemastix (available from many drugstores)

CAUTION: Be sure to wash your hands thoroughly after handling raw meat.

Procedure

1. Use the eyedropper to place 1 drop of red watercolor paint, 1 drop of ketchup, and 1 drop of blood on the plate.

2. Add a drop of water to each red drop to make sure that they do not dry out.

3. Put a Hemastix strip in each solution. What happens? What color does the Hemastix strip turn in each solution? What color indicates blood?

The Hemastix changes color in blood. A Hemastix strip contains chemicals that will react with the chemicals normally found in blood. This simple test is often done at the scene of a crime as a quick way to determine whether a substance is blood. Later, samples are tested in the laboratory to confirm the field test. Other tests, such as blood-typing or DNA profiling (see Chapter 4, Project 4, DNA Testing), give more detailed information about the blood and the individual it came from.

A ransom note is important evidence in a kidnapping investigation. If forensic investigators can identify the pen that wrote the note, they may be able to link the note to a suspect. There are several ways to identify the type of pen used to write a ransom note or other criminal communication. Try the following activity to investigate one way to identify ink and the pen it came from.

Materials

scissors

coffee filters

ruler

water-soluble felt-tipped
   pens of different brands
   and different colors

drinking glass

tap water

paper towel

Procedure

1. Cut the coffee filters into several strips 1 inch (2.5 cm) wide.

2. Make a thick circle with one felt-tipped pen about 1 inch (2.5 cm) from the end of one strip.

3. Pour water into the drinking glass so that it fills ½ inch (1 cm) of the bottom of the glass.

4. Dip the end of the strip in the water so that the water covers about ½ inch (1 cm) of the end of the strip that you marked. The water should not touch the circle you drew.

5. Watch the water creep up the strip until it reaches the top of the strip.

6. Take the strip out of the water and place it on the paper towel. Above the filter, write the name of the color of the pen on the paper towel, using the same pen you used on the strip.

7. Repeat the experiment with the rest of the strips and pens.

8. Observe what happened to the circles made on the strips. What do you notice about the dyes in the pens?

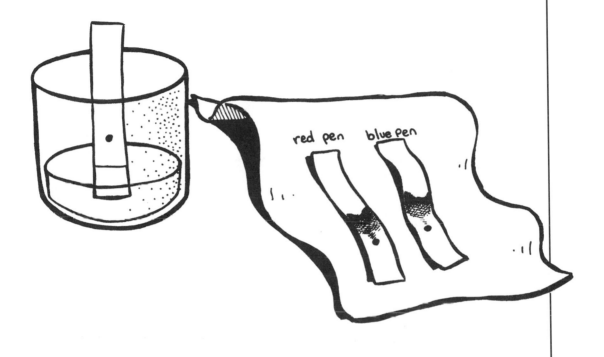

red pen   blue pen

Ink is a complex chemical made up of several chemicals. Through a process called **chromatography**, complex chemicals like ink are separated into the chemicals of which they are made.

In this activity you performed an ink chromatography test. The colors of the inks separated in different patterns because the ink colors are carried by the water at different speeds.

A forensic scientist can compare the chromatography pattern of the ink used to write a note with the chromatography patterns of several different known pens. This allows him or her to identify which pen was used to write the note.

PROJECT 5
Burned Documents

Even a note that has been completely burned can be important evidence in an investigation. Try the following activity to restore and read a burned document.

Materials

ballpoint pen
sheet of white paper
metal pie pan
matches (to be used only by an adult)
cookie sheet

½ cup (125 ml) glycerin (available from most drugstores)
1½ cup (375 ml) tap water
spray bottle
adult helper

Procedure

NOTE: This activity requires adult help.

1. Write the message "Robbery set for 3:00 P.M. on Thursday" on the white paper.

2. Crumple the paper into a ball and place it in the middle of the pie pan.

3. Have your adult helper use the matches to set the paper on fire.

4. Allow the fire to burn out and cool down. When the burned paper is cool, carefully transfer it to the cookie sheet.

5. Observe the burned paper. Can you still see any of the writing on the paper?

6. Mix the glycerin with the water and place the mixture in the spray bottle.

7. Carefully spray the burned paper with the mixture until the paper is completely wet. Gently unfold the crumpled paper and flatten it on the cookie sheet. Use more spray if necessary.

8. Observe the paper. Can you now read any of the writing?

A document may be burned either by accident or on purpose. Either way, handling a charred or burned document is one of the most difficult tasks a crime lab can face. The documents must be transferred to the crime lab with the utmost care and are often hand delivered in a cotton- or wool-lined box. Once the document is in the lab, the forensic scientist begins the careful process of reading it.

First, the forensic scientist must flatten the burned document without causing it to fall apart. The glycerin-and-water solution used in this activity softened the burned paper so that you could flatten it. Forensic scientists use a similar procedure. They float burned sheets in a large tray containing a mixture of glycerin, alcohol, and a chemical called choral hydrate to soften the paper.

Once the document is flattened, the forensic scientist tries to read it. Most ballpoint pen inks contain a small amount of metal in the dyes. These metals are able to survive fire, so anything written with a ballpoint pen can be seen when the paper is flattened. The forensic scientist then photographs the document as evidence.

If the writing on the document is not easily visible, the forensic scientist will sometimes photograph the burned document with special film called infrared film. This film enhances the writing on the document and helps make it more visible.

4

Living Proof

Using Biology to Learn More about a Crime

After the chemistry department, the biology department is the second largest unit in most forensic laboratories. **Biology** is the study of **organisms** (living things). To many people, the biology department *is* the forensic laboratory. The biology department does tests that deal with organisms and the clues they give to help solve a crime.

Forensic scientists in this department may be specialists in the fields of **botany** (the study of plants), **zoology** (the study of animals), **anatomy** and **physiology** (the study of the structure and function of organisms, especially humans), or **anthropology** (the study of humans, especially their physical characteristics and social relationships). Forensic scientists use biology to determine time of death, to identify and match blood samples, and to examine hair, fibers, and other trace evidence. They even study dirt to help solve crimes! Try the following activities to see the many ways that biology is used to crack criminal cases.

PROJECT 1
Teeth Impressions

Teeth and teeth impressions can be used in an investigation to identify an unknown person and to learn information about him or her. Try the following activity to learn more about what teeth can tell you.

Materials

scissors   marking pen
Styrofoam plate

1. Cut the Styrofoam plate into six equal wedges.

2. Stack two of the wedges together, and cut 1 inch (2.5 cm) from the pointed end of both. Throw away the pieces that you cut off.

3. Slip the cut ends of the two wedges into your mouth. Push them in as far as possible while still being comfortable.

4. Bite down on the wedges firmly, then remove them.

5. Label the top wedge Impression of the Top Teeth and the bottom wedge Impression of the Bottom Teeth.

6. Examine the teeth impressions. How many teeth made marks in the top impression? How many made marks in the bottom impression? What features of the impressions are useful in telling the top teeth from the bottom teeth? How are the teeth different?

Collect teeth impressions from several helpers. Be sure to label each impression with the person's name whether it is the top or bottom teeth. Leave the room, then have one helper take a bite from a piece of cheese or hard chocolate. Can you identify who took the bite by comparing the impression in the cheese or chocolate to the set of impressions?

More Fun Stuff to Do

E x p l a n a t i o n

Humans are provided with two sets of teeth, which appear at different times in life. The first set, called **deciduous teeth**, appear when we are children. The second and final set, the **permanent teeth**, appear later and replace the deciduous teeth.

This process of replacement begins at about age six, when we lose our front incisor teeth, and continues to about age eighteen, when we get our third set of molars, commonly called our wisdom teeth. We have twenty deciduous teeth: four incisors and two canines (which cut or tear food) and four molars (which chew and grind food) in each jaw. We have thirty-two permanent teeth: four incisors, two canines, four premolars, and six molars in each jaw.

PERMANENT TEETH

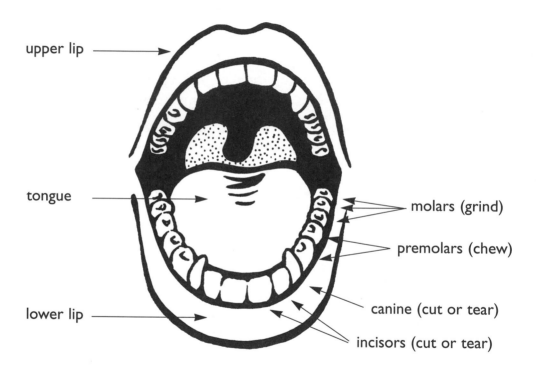

upper lip

tongue

lower lip

molars (grind)

premolars (chew)

canine (cut or tear)

incisors (cut or tear)

The arrangement of each person's teeth is unique and can be easily used to help identify a person. The number and type of teeth are valuable in determining the age of the individual. Forensic dentists can compare teeth impressions to dental records. Eighty percent of the time, teeth impressions are used to identify unknown victims.

Detective Science *in Action*

Teeth impressions have been used to identify many criminals. One hungry burglar was caught because of a half-eaten piece of cheese he left at the scene of the crime. The burglar became hungry during a break-in and took a piece of cheese out of the refrigerator. He had just taken one bite from the cheese when he heard a noise. Startled, be dropped the cheese and ran out of the house. When police arrived, they found the cheese. They later matched the teeth impressions of the suspect to the bite marks in the cheese.

PROJECT 2
Bone Identification

Bones can tell a great deal about the life of people who died. They can give hints about their ancestry, sex, age, and **stature** (height), and often they help identify someone. Bones in a criminal investigation can give clues about the time and manner of death. Try the following activities to learn more about bones and what they can tell you.

Materials

2 stockpots, one with lid
tap water
whole chicken
timer
tongs

platter
½ cup (125 ml) baking soda
scrub brush
adult helper

NOTE: This activity requires adult help.

1. Fill one stockpot halfway with water. Put the chicken in the pot and cover it with the lid.

2. Have your adult helper set the pot on the stove burner, set the heat to medium, and boil the chicken for 2 hours.

3. Have your adult helper use the tongs to transfer the chicken from the pot to the platter. Let the chicken cool. When the chicken is cool, remove as much meat from the bones as possible.

   NOTE: Have your adult helper save the good parts of the meat for a meal.

4. Fill the second pot halfway with water. Add the bones and the baking soda.

5. Ask your adult helper to boil the bones for 1 hour. This should remove all remaining meat from the bones.

6. Allow the water to cool, then transfer the bones to the platter. Use the scrub brush to clean the bones.

7. Examine the bones. How are they alike? How are they different? If you were given only one bone from the chicken, would you know where in the chicken it came from?

8. Use the diagram to help you reconstruct the chicken skeleton.

Explanation

Forensic anthropologists study the bones of the dead. They use the same techniques and discoveries to help solve twentieth-century crimes as other anthropologists use to unveil the secrets of ancient civilizations. Indeed, many of the nation's forensic anthropologists spend much of their time digging into remains of ancient times.

CHICKEN SKELETON

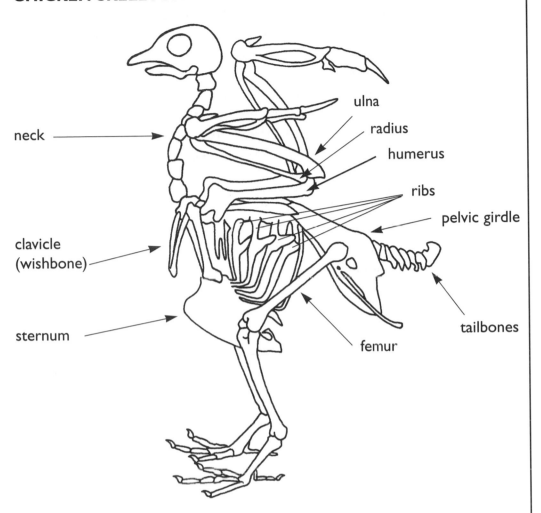

One of the first things that a forensic anthropologist must determine is whether a bone is human or animal. This is often more difficult than it sounds. Some other mammals have bones very similar to human bones. For example, the bones in a bear paw look almost exactly like the bones in a human hand. Investigators also need to know whether bones are recent or ancient. This will help them determine whether the bone comes from a place of historical significance or the scene of a crime.

The skull can be used to help re-create what a person looked like. Forensic sculptors use computers to help put flesh and skin on a skeleton and thus match a skull to a photograph of a missing person. These same techniques have been used to give other anthropologists an idea of what dinosaurs looked like.

The skeleton can give many important details about a person, including his or her occupation. For example, the bones of waiters and tennis players show signs of arm strength, with greater development on their strong side. Male **pelvic bones** (the bones that form the hips) are different from those of the female. Men's pelvic bones are narrow and steep while women's are shallower and broader. Forensic anthropologists often use the features of the eye sockets and nose cavity to categorize people in one or more continental or ancestral groups.

One of the best collaborative efforts in the science world is that between the Smithsonian Institution's Department of Anthropology and the FBI in Washington, D.C. Here, pure science and hard-nosed police work team up to help solve some of the most tantalizing mysteries of humanity's past and present.

PROJECT 3
Feet and Inches

Even the bones of the feet can tell you a lot about the person they came from. Try the following investigation to see what feet reveal about a person's height.

Materials

tape measure
pen or pencil
paper

calculator
several helpers

Procedure

NOTE: This activity works best if the helpers are older people who have stopped growing, rather than young children.

1. Have each helper remove his or her shoes. Use the tape measure to measure the height of each helper in inches (cm). Write each person's name and height on the paper.

2. Have each helper stand with his or her left heel against the wall and perpendicular to the wall.

3. Carefully measure the length in inches (cm) of each person's left foot, from the wall to the tip of the big toe. Write that information next to each person's name and height.

4. Look at the numbers. Do you notice a pattern?

5. Use the calculator to divide the length of each person's left foot by his or her height. Multiply the result by 100. What results do you get?

Have a helper stretch his or her arms out sideways as far as they can go. Measure the distance from the tip of the middle finger on one hand to the tip of the middle finger on the other. Compare that measurement to your helper's height. What do you notice?

Explanation

The results of your calculations in step 5 should all have been approximately 15. For example, if a person is 63 inches (160 cm) tall and his or her left foot is 9½ inches (24 cm) long, the result would be 9½ inches (24 cm) divided by 63 inches (160 cm) times 100 equals 15. This means that the length of a person's foot is about 15 percent of his or her height.

If a forensic scientist had to identify a person using only the bones of the foot, he or she could approximate the height of that individual using this technique. This is because the bones in the body grow at certain rates and are in proportion to one another.

Thus, in the More Fun Stuff to Do section, the distance between the tips of the middle fingers when the arms are outstretched is the same as a person's height. As a person grows taller, the feet grow bigger and the arms grow longer at the same time. By the time he or she is full grown, foot length and arm span will give approximate values for height.

These values are not always true as people grow. The ratio of one body part to another will change greatly throughout childhood. For example, the circumference of the head of a newborn is about 25 percent of the baby's height, while that of an adult is only about half that value.

PROJECT 4
DNA Testing

If cells, such as blood cells, are found at the scene of a crime, forensic scientists can perform a test called **DNA profiling** to attempt to link the cells to a certain suspect. DNA profiling is one of the most important discoveries in recent scientific history. DNA profiles look similar to the bar codes found on the products we buy. Try the following activity to simulate how DNA profiles are compared.

Materials

bar codes shown

Procedure

1. Observe the bar codes shown.
2. Match the mystery bar code to bar codes A through D.

MYSTERY BAR CODE

BAR CODES

Explanation

The mystery bar code is identical to bar code C. Just as bar codes contain information about the identification of a product, DNA profiles contain coded information about the makeup of a human being. **DNA** (*d*eoxyribo*n*ucleic *a*cid) is basically the blueprint or recipe for the human body. DNA is located in the **nucleus** (center) of every human cell. Every cell in the human body has 46 **chromosomes**, which contain coded information arranged into groups called **genes.** This coded information is a person's DNA. Each person's DNA is unique, so only very small samples are required for analysis.

DNA analysis, which can be done by the crime lab or an independent laboratory, is a complicated procedure. It involves the following steps:

1. DNA is removed from the cell nucleus.

2. The DNA strands are separated from the rest of the cell parts and chopped into smaller pieces.

3. The human DNA pieces are combined with radioactive DNA. This allows the forensic scientist to track the pieces of human DNA later.

4. The DNA pieces are separated from one another into bands according to size, using **gel electrophoresis**, a process similar to chromatography. (See Chapter 3, Project 4, Ink Identification, for more information about chromatography.)

5. X rays are taken of the separated DNA pieces (the radioactive DNA will be easily seen on the X ray) to record the individual's DNA profile.

Just as you compared bar codes, forensic scientists can compare a DNA profile obtained from cells found at a crime scene to the DNA profile of a known suspect, to determine whether the suspect was at the scene of the crime. Examples of DNA profiles are shown.

We hear in the news about forensic experts performing DNA tests in spectacular court cases. However, the greatest number of DNA tests are routinely conducted to establish the identity of a father or a child, or to prove or disprove family relationships in immigration applications.

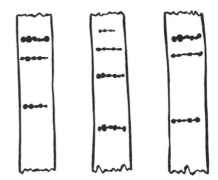

PROJECT 5
Microbes

Our bodies carry organisms that are too small to see. These tiny creatures, called **microbes**, can be used to identify whether a suspect wore certain clothing or whether he or she was at the scene of a crime.

Materials

½ cup (125 ml) tap water

saucepan

4 packages of unflavored gelatin

timer

clean 1-quart (1-liter) jar with lid

trash can

tennis shoes

cotton swab

rubber gloves

dishwashing liquid

adult helper

Procedure

NOTE: This is an outdoor activity and requires adult help.

1. Have your adult helper prepare the gelatin by boiling the water in the saucepan and dissolving the gelatin packages in the boiling water.

2. Allow the gelatin to cool until it is cool enough to handle but not solid (about 5 minutes).

3. When the gelatin has cooled, pour it into the jar.

4. Hold the jar over the trash can. Tip the jar on its side and let the excess gelatin pour out.

5. Set the jar on its side and leave it undisturbed for 4 hours.

6. Put the tennis shoes on without socks and go play outside for at least 30 minutes.

7. Remove the shoes. Take the cotton swab and rub it between all your toes.

8. Reach into the jar and carefully brush the gelatin with the cotton swab so that you make a wavy line in the gelatin as shown.

9. Wash your hands and feet.

10. Place the lid on the jar and put the jar in a warm, dark location. Leave it there for 4 days.

11. After 4 days, observe the gelatin in the jar. What do you see?

CAUTION: Do not touch the gelatin! Don't keep the jar longer than four days.

12. When you are done with the experiment, put on the rubber gloves, fill the jar with hot water, let it soak for 5 minutes, and then wash the jar. The gelatin will dissolve and can be washed down the sink.

CAUTION: Be sure to wash your hands thoroughly when you are finished.

Explanation

The inside of your shoes is warm, dark, and damp from sweat. This is a perfect environment for microbes to grow, as they like warm, dark, damp places. Your jar had a similar environment. The gelatin provided food for the microbes that were on your feet. Having food and a nice place to live allowed the microbes to eat and reproduce.

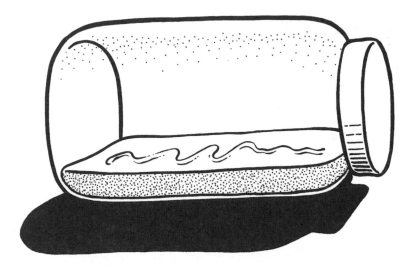

After four days, you should have been able to see grooves in the gelatin where the microbes had eaten it. Sometimes you might have seen different colors, depending on the type of microbe that was living on your feet and on the gelatin. If you could look at microbes under a microscope, you would see that they have unique characteristics, such as size, shape, color, and reaction to certain chemicals.

Microbes can be found not only on the inside of shoes, but on the soles of shoes and your skin as well. Forensic scientists compare microbes found at a crime scene to known microbes and to those found on a suspect. If the microbes match, they can be used to place the suspect at the crime scene.

PROJECT 6
Seeds and Spores

Small seeds found on a suspect's clothes or in a vehicle driven by the suspect can be important clues to where that person has been. Try the following activity to see how this type of information is used to solve crimes.

Materials

a pair of old wool socks

field with weeds or bushes

white paper

magnifying lens

Procedure

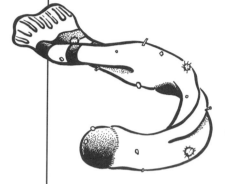

NOTE: This is an outdoor activity.

1. Put the wool socks on over your shoes and walk around in the field.

2. Remove the socks and observe them. You should find many seeds stuck to the socks.

3. At home, pick off the seeds from the socks and put them on the white paper. Observe the seeds with the magnifying lens. How many different types of seeds did you collect?

4. Group the seeds so that similar ones are together. Can you guess which plants the seeds came from?

More Fun Stuff to Do

1 Plant the seeds you collected to see what kind of plants will sprout. To make sure the seeds will sprout, before planting them place them in a plastic bag in the refrigerator for a week. (Most seeds in the wild are used to going through a cold winter before sprouting.) You can either remove the seeds from the socks and plant them in a pot filled with soil or fill the socks with soil, water them, and place the soil-filled socks on an old plate. Create your own Chia socks!

2 Repeat the original activity in a different field with different socks. Compare the seeds found in each field. How are they different? Can you tell by looking at the seeds found on the socks which field they came from?

3 Repeat the original activity in a different season of the year. Compare the seeds found in each season. How are they different?

Explanation

The kinds of plants that grow in a particular area are determined by several factors, such as soil type, amount of water, and temperature. Most plants go through a growth cycle each year. In the spring, the plants sprout, begin growing, and then bloom, or flower. They continue to grow rapidly in the summer. In the autumn, the plants get ready for their quiet period. Grasses and many weeds release seeds into the air or onto the ground in preparation for the next spring. During the winter, the plants are dormant, meaning that they are alive but asleep. In the spring, seeds will sprout and the cycle begins again.

Seeds come from complex plants like grasses, bushes, and trees. Simple plants like bacteria, algae, mosses, and ferns produce **spores**, which are small cells that can develop into a new individual.

Using seeds and spores can be an effective way to help identify where a suspect has been walking and to link him or her to the scene of a crime. For example, if seeds found stuck to a suspect's socks match seeds from grasses near a warehouse robbery, the evidence shows that the suspect had the opportunity to commit the crime.

PROJECT 7
Dust and Dirt

Dust, dirt, and soil can be important evidence in an investigation. Try the following activity to see how dirt can be used to solve a crime.

Materials

dirt from three locations
plastic bags
marking pen

3 sheets of white paper
magnifying lens

Procedure

NOTE: This is an outdoor activity.

1. Collect dirt from three locations. Place it in the plastic bags and mark the location on each bag.

2. At home, place a dirt sample from each bag on separate sheets of white paper. Examine the samples with the magnifying lens.

3. How are the dirt samples different? Is the soil light or dark? What does the soil look like? What size are the grains in the soil? Do you see any stones? Is there any decaying plant material in the soil? What characteristics could you use to identify the dirt from a particular place?

Explanation

Soil is one-half air and water, both of which are necessary for plants and animals to live. The rest of soil consists of recycling organisms—such as fungi, molds, bacteria, and earthworms—pieces of rock, and **humus** (decaying plant and animal matter). The size of the soil particles determines whether soil is sand, silt, or clay. Sand has the largest soil particles and clay has the smallest.

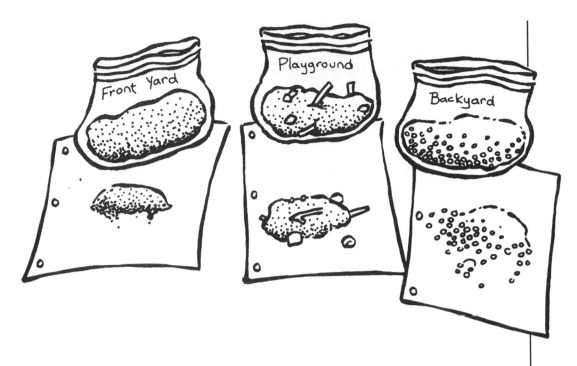

All this information can be used to study soil samples found at a crime scene. Dust and dirt are common as trace evidence because they are easily carried from the scene of a crime in the soles of shoes, on clothing, or on the tires of a vehicle. Forensic scientists compare the dust and dirt found at a crime scene with selected samples to determine where they came from.

Detective Science *in Action*

In 1977, Janie Sheperd had been missing for four days. Her car, discovered on a London street, had been driven roughly 75 miles (120 km) from her home. By analyzing thick deposits of mud found underneath the vehicle, investigators determined that the car had been driven in one of four surrounding counties, which greatly narrowed the search area.

Very small plants and animals called **microorganisms** are found on land and in water. Like microbes, seeds, and spores, microorganisms can be important in an investigation. Try the following activity to investigate microorganisms that are found in water.

Materials

large glass jar with lid   magnifying lens

water from a pond or lake   microscope (optional)

Procedure

NOTE: This is an outdoor activity.

1. Use the jar to collect some water from a pond or lake, then put the lid on the jar.

2. At home, use the magnifying lens or microscope to examine the water for microorganisms. How many different microorganisms can you find?

    NOTE: Many of the microorganisms are clear or light-colored and are very small, so you will have to look carefully. They may appear to be small specks that move!

Small plants and animals that live in water are the foundation of all life. These microorganisms are eaten by larger organisms, which in turn are eaten by still larger organisms. This food chain allows many different organisms to live on earth.

Microorganisms found in water can give valuable information to a detective. Microorganisms called **diatoms** (microscopic algae that contain a sandlike substance called silica in their cell walls) are very important. The presence or absence of diatoms in a dead body found in water can tell forensic scientists whether the victim drowned or died before entering the water. When death is caused by drowning in natural water, such as lakes and rivers, the water in the body, especially that in the lungs but even water in the bloodstream, will contain diatoms. If the victim was already dead when the body entered the water, no diatoms will be found.

In investigations in which a body is found in a different location from where it drowned, forensic scientists study diatoms to determine with considerable accuracy the area of origin. This is because there are over 15,000 species of diatoms, and any combination of them found in a sample is likely to be unique.

PROJECT 9
Heat Loss

There are many times that the temperature of an object plays an important role in solving a crime. Heat from the engine of an automobile may indicate that it has just been driven. A warm cup of coffee on a kitchen table may mean that a suspect has just left. The temperature of a body can indicate to detectives when a death has occurred. Try the following activity to see how temperature can be used by forensic scientists.

Materials

2 cups (500 ml) of hot coffee

coffee cup

thermometer (measures
up to 212°F [100°C])

stopwatch or watch with
second hand

pen or pencil

notebook

adult helper

Procedure

NOTE: This activity requires adult help. Have your adult helper keep the hot coffee at the same temperature throughout the experiment by placing it on a stove or hot plate.

1. Have your adult helper pour 1 cup (250 ml) of the hot coffee into the coffee cup.

2. Put the thermometer in the coffee, start your stopwatch, and record the temperature of the coffee in your notebook.

3. Continue to record the temperature of the coffee at 1-minute intervals until the temperature no longer changes. Empty the cup of coffee.

4. Leave the room. Have the adult helper pour another cup of hot coffee into the coffee cup and note the time that he or she pours the coffee.

5. Have the adult helper wait several minutes before inviting you back into the room.

6. Take the temperature of the coffee. Compare the temperature to your records. How many minutes has it been since your helper poured the coffee into the cup?

158°F ≈ 70°C

When an object is removed from a source of heat, its temperature begins to drop. It cools rather rapidly until it reaches the temperature of the surrounding air, at which point its temperature stabilizes. The heat loss of the same size of object at the same initial temperature occurs at the same rate each time. This allows one to determine, with some degree of accuracy, the time that the object was removed from the heat source. In this activity, as long as the same amount of coffee at the same initial temperature was poured the second time, and as long as the room temperature did not change, you should have been able to estimate the time the coffee was poured.

At death, a body stops generating heat and its temperature drops gradually. At first the cooling is relatively rapid—approximately 1.5°F (0.8°C) per hour—but this rate slows after a few hours. In addition to size, initial temperature, and the temperature of the surroundings, body type will also affect the cooling rate. A thin body will cool more rapidly than a heavier one. By taking a body's temperature, a forensic scientist can estimate the time of death.

PROJECT 10
Decomposition

Decomposition is the natural process of decay. Often, the decomposition of materials surrounding a body can give a forensic scientist valuable information. Not all materials decompose at the same rate. **Organic** material, which is material from plants or animals, decomposes differently from **inorganic**, or man-made, material. Forensic scientists can study the state of decomposition of these materials to approximate time of death. Try this activity to learn how materials can decompose at different rates and how that information can help solve crimes.

Materials

clear plastic 2-quart (2-liter) soda bottle

scissors

cheesecloth

rubber band

tape

2 cups (500 ml) sand

2 quarts (2 liters) garden soil (from an outdoor location)

organic material, such as leaves, twigs, grass, shredded newspaper, and pine needles

inorganic material, such as Styrofoam, plastic, and scraps of fabric or leather

pen or pencil

notebook

rubber gloves

several sheets of newspaper

stick

worms (optional)

tap water

adult helper

Procedure

NOTE: This activity requires adult help.

1. Remove the label as best you can from the plastic soda bottle.

2. Have your adult helper cut the bottle into two sections, making the cut approximately one-third of the way from the bottom.

3. Cover the mouth of the bottle with cheesecloth and secure it with the rubber band.

4. Turn the top section of the bottle upside down and place it in the bottom section as shown. Tape the two sections together.

5. Put the sand in the upside-down container. Place a 1-cup (250-ml) layer of the garden soil on top of the sand.

6. Look at the organic and inorganic materials. Which items do you think will decompose quickly? Why? Which items do you think will take longer to decompose? Why? Record your predictions in your notebook.

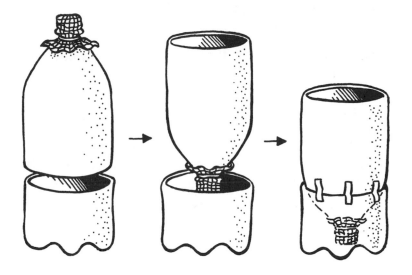

7. Add a small amount of each organic and inorganic material to the container, then add another layer of soil. Continue to layer organic and inorganic materials and soil until they reach the top of the container. Add more materials on top of the last layer of soil.

8. Add worms to the container, if you like.

9. Pour water into the container until it starts to drip through the cheesecloth.

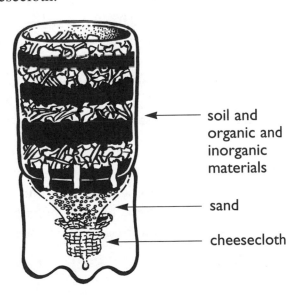

soil and organic and inorganic materials

sand

cheesecloth

10. Set the container where it will not be disturbed for a month. Water the container twice a week.

11. Observe the container every other day. Record your observations.

12. After a month, put on the rubber gloves and pour the contents of the container onto the newspaper. Use the stick to move the soil around. Observe the condition of the organic and inorganic materials. Were your predictions correct?

CAUTION: Always wear rubber gloves when examining the experiment materials. Return worms to the earth and throw out the rest of the project when you are finished. Be sure to wash your hands thoroughly when you are done.

Explanation

Decomposition is nature's way to recycle organic, or living, material. Organic material is broken down into nutrients that can be reused by plants as they grow. Some inorganic, or non-living, material is broken down as well, but usually at a slower rate. Bacteria, fungi, worms, and microorganisms all help to break down these materials.

Worms in particular help to speed up the process of decomposition. They make extensive networks of tunnels that help air and water reach the roots of plants. The tunnels also provide air and water for other soil-dwelling insects and small organisms that help with the process of decomposition. Worms also turn the soil by moving deep soil up to the surface and by dragging plant materials underground. One cup (250 ml) of soil may contain more than 5 billion living creatures!

Forensic scientists use their knowledge of the decomposition rates of various substances to help solve crimes in several ways. For example, the state of decomposition of a letter found behind a house could link a suspect to the time of a robbery, while a rotting apple core could be an important clue for police looking for a lost camper.

5

Paper Trail

Analyzing Documents to Solve Crimes

One of the oldest methods of forensic science is to study written materials that relate to crimes. As far back as ancient Rome, handwriting comparisons were used as evidence in court. There were handwriting experts in ancient Rome as there are today. In addition to handwritten evidence, there are many other ways documents can be involved in crimes. Try the following activities to investigate several ways forensic scientists analyze documents.

PROJECT I
Indented Paper

If another piece of paper is directly under the piece that is written on, the paper underneath will pick up an impression of the writing. This can be valuable evidence for a detective who is looking for clues in a missing-person case or trying to match the origin of a ransom note in a kidnapping case. Try the following activity to see how this technique is done.

Materials

several sheets of white paper   lamp or other light source

ballpoint pen   pencil

Procedure

1. Stack the paper. Use the ballpoint pen to write an address or a phone number on the top sheet of paper.

2. Remove the top sheet, then hold the second sheet of paper up to the lamp. Can you see anything?

3. Lay the second sheet flat. Use the edge of the pencil lead to lightly shade over the place where the writing was made. Can you read the address or phone number on the second sheet?

Repeat the experiment, using different types and amounts of paper, and exerting either more or less pressure while writing. Do these changes affect your ability to read the writing on the second sheet of paper?

Explanation

How well the impression can be read will depend on a number of factors, such as the thickness of the paper, whether the sheets were on a hard or a soft surface, and the amount of pressure exerted by the writer.

If an indented sheet is found as evidence at a crime scene, this technique can be used to match it to a threatening letter or a ransom note. If a diary or a business ledger with pages torn out is found, this technique can also be used to determine what was written on the missing pages.

PROJECT 2
Typewriting Analysis

If a criminal communicates using a typewriter or a computer printer, it may be possible to identify which machine was used. A typed letter demanding blackmail money or instructing someone where to find a kidnapping victim could be traced back to a suspect's typewriter or computer printer. Try the following activity to investigate how detectives analyze typewriting to solve crimes.

pencil

paper with typing on it from several sources, such as papers your friends and family members have typed using different typewriters and computers

scissors

glue

3-by-5-inch (7.5-by-12.5-cm) index cards

magnifying lens

Procedure

1. Use the pencil to number all of the typed pages you've collected.

2. Use the scissors to cut several words out of each page. Glue the words on the index cards, using a separate card for words taken from each page.

3. Record the number of the page the words came from on each card.

4. Use the magnifying lens to observe the words on each card. What do you notice about each? Compare the same letter, such as *e* or *a*, on each card. How are the letters different?

Detective Science in Action

Detective Science in Action

Detective Science in Action

Detective Science in Action

Detective Science in Action

Detective Science in Action

Detective Science in Action

---

ave a helper cut a word from one of the pages while you look away. Try to determine which page the word came from by comparing it to your sample cards.

Explanation

Few people write letters on typewriters today. Word processors, computers, and printers have made writing letters much easier. Even so, there are differences between how a letter is made by each machine. By looking carefully at those differences, detectives can determine which machine wrote a certain letter.

Detective Science *in Action*

In a famous spy case in 1950, Alger Hiss was brought to trial for passing secret documents to the Soviet Union. Hiss was convicted of **perjury** (lying while under oath), largely because of the evidence that involved his typewriter. Typed documents taken from a Soviet spy contained valuable information from the U.S. State Department. The typing on these documents matched Hiss's typewriter, which had rather unusual print. The prosecution claimed that Hiss had used the typewriter to copy State Department documents that were later given to secret agents from the Soviet Union.

PROJECT 3
Top-of-Letter Handwriting Analysis

Each person's style of handwriting is unique and can be identified, often even if a person is trying to disguise his or her handwriting. Try the following activity to see one way handwriting is analyzed.

Materials

pen or sharp pencil

sheet of white paper

sheet of tracing paper

ruler

Procedure

1. Write your name two times on the sheet of white paper.

2. Place the tracing paper over your signature.

3. Make a small mark on the tracing paper at all of the high points of each letter in each signature.

4. Use the ruler to join each mark to the one next to it, creating a zigzag line across the top of each signature.

5. Make a top-of-letter analysis by comparing the two zigzag lines. Are they similar?

102

Write your name on another sheet of paper. Have a helper **forge** (copy with the intent to deceive) your signature 1 to 2 inches (2.5 to 5 cm) below your real signature. Make a top-of-the-letter analysis of the two signatures. How do they compare? Could this method of handwriting analysis prove that your helper's signature was forged?

Explanation

An individual's handwriting depends on several things, such as the brain, the eye, and the hand of the individual. It is affected by a person's physical and emotional well-being, the position in which he or she is writing, and circumstances that might influence speed. Normally, a person's handwriting will be slightly different from signature to signature. So, if a series of signatures on checks are exactly the same, it may indicate that someone forged the signatures by copying or tracing them. If the signatures are *very* different, however, this can also indicate that the signatures are fakes.

A signature is often all that is needed to withdraw money from a bank account, to write a check, or to make a purchase with a credit card. These are the most common situations in which **forgery**, the act of falsifying documents, occurs. Every year, millions of dollars are lost to forgeries. Forgeries are found by comparing the signature in question with a known example of a person's handwriting. For example, banks and credit card companies keep a file of copies of their customers' signatures, and if they think that a check or credit slip might be a forgery, they will compare the signature in question with the signature in their files. If the signatures are different, they will call the police for a complete investigation. Forensic scientists will then do an even more thorough analysis of the signatures.

The next three projects are variations on top-of-letter handwriting analysis.

Another way to analyze handwriting is to analyze the bottom of the letters.

Materials

pen or sharp pencil

sheet of white paper

sheet of tracing paper

ruler

Procedure

1. Write your name two times on the sheet of white paper.

2. Place the tracing paper over your signature.

3. Make a small mark on the tracing paper at all of the low points of each letter in each signature.

4. Use the ruler to join each mark to the one next to it, creating a zigzag line across the bottom of each signature.

5. Compare the two zigzag lines. Are they similar?

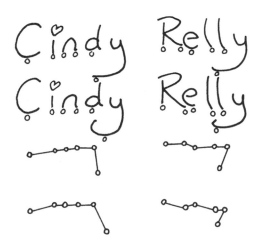

Write your name on another sheet of paper. Have a helper forge your signature below your real signature. Make a bottom-of-the-letter analysis. How do the two signatures compare? Could this method of handwriting analysis prove that your helper's signature was forged?

More Fun Stuff to Do

PROJECT 5
Spacing Analysis

Experts also compare the spacing between words and letters to analyze and identify handwriting. Try a spacing analysis to see how this technique is done.

Materials

pen or sharp pencil
sheet of white paper

sheet of tracing paper
ruler

Procedure

1. Write your name two times on the sheet of white paper.

2. Place the tracing paper over your signature.

3. Make a small mark on the tracing paper at all of the low points of the beginning and ending of each letter in each signature.

4. Use the ruler to join the rightmost mark of each letter to the leftmost mark of the next letter for each signature, creating a series of short lines between the letters.

5. Compare the two sets of lines. Are they similar?

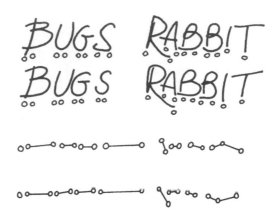

Write your name on another sheet of paper. Have a helper forge your signature below your real signature. Make a spacing analysis. How do the two signatures compare? Could this method of handwriting analysis prove that your helper's signature was forged?

PROJECT 6
Slant Analysis

The slant of a signature is another way to compare handwriting. Perform your own slant analysis to master the technique.

Materials

pen or sharp pencil

sheet of white paper

sheet of tracing paper

ruler

Procedure

1. Write your name two times on the sheet of white paper.

2. Place the tracing paper over your signature.

3. Use the ruler to make a slash through each letter in each signature so that each slash has the same slant as the letter.

4. Compare the two series of slanted lines. Are they similar?

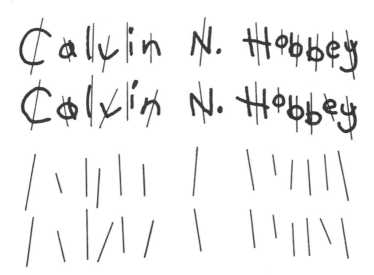

More Fun Stuff to Do

Write your name on another sheet of paper. Have a helper forge your signature below your real signature. Make a slant analysis. How do the two signatures compare? Could this method of handwriting analysis prove that your helper's signature was forged?

Explanation

All four methods of handwriting analysis—top-of-letter, bottom-of-letter, spacing, and slant—help forensic scientists examine and compare handwritten documents. Often, forensic scientists perform several forms of analysis on the same handwriting to confirm that it is a forgery. These methods can be done more accurately by using computers. A sample signature can be scanned and placed in the computer's memory for later comparison.

Detective Science *in Action*

One of the most famous kidnapping cases in the United States happened in 1932 when the baby son of Colonel and Mrs. Charles Lindbergh was kidnapped. Colonel Lindbergh was the first person to make a solo airplane flight across the Atlantic and was widely considered a hero. The conviction of Bruno Richard Hauptman, arrested for kidnapping the Lindbergh baby, was based in part on the testimony of handwriting experts. They compared the writing on the ransom note with handwriting samples that the police obtained from Hauptman after his arrest.

PROJECT 7
Counterfeiting

We all know what a dollar bill looks like, but how many of us have really examined one carefully? Try the following activity to investigate how fake bills, called **counterfeit** bills, are detected.

Materials

picture of counterfeit
  bill on the next page
$1 bill

pencil
paper

Procedure

1. There are at least twelve things wrong with the $1 bill on the next page. Examine the picture and see how many errors you can find. Write down your answers.

2. After you have found as many errors as you can, compare the picture to the real $1 bill. Write down any additional errors you notice.

3. Compare your answers with the list on the next page. Did you find the twelve errors listed?

Explanation

Shown on the next page are twelve of the mistakes on the bill.

To **counterfeit** means to make a copy of something with the intent to trick or deceive. It used to be very difficult to counterfeit paper money. The counterfeiter had to make special plates, or replicas, of each side of the bill being counterfeited. There were many places where mistakes could be made. The wrong hair on the president or an error in the serial number could ruin months of work.

With the rise of color copiers, however, counterfeiting money is now easier. New high-speed, high-quality laser copiers are a quick and simple way to duplicate money. To combat counterfeiting on this new generation of copiers, the U.S. government is now printing money on special paper that can't be purchased by anyone but the government. Counterfeit money will not only look different, but feel different, too. The Canadian government has begun using a high-tech solution to stop counterfeiting. They've started placing holograms on their money, similar to the ones on credit cards.

There are many documents besides paper money that can be counterfeited. With the aid of copiers, payroll and other checks are commonly forged. But even nonpaper items, such as credit cards, can be copied. As with money, holograms have been added to credit cards to make them harder to forge. And special dyes that can only be seen under ultraviolet light are used to add pictures and words to the front of the credit card.

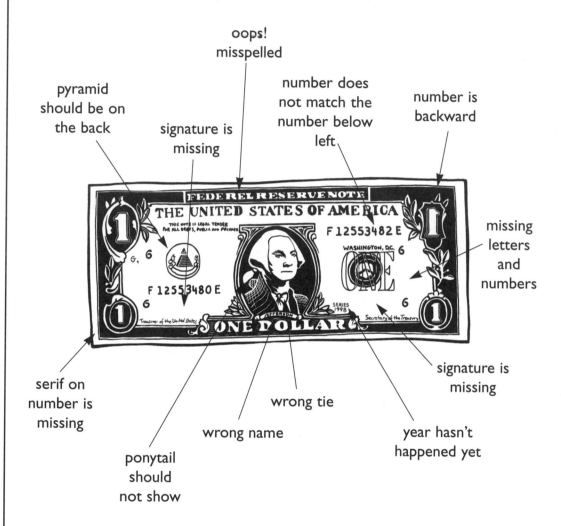

Glossary

accomplice   A partner in crime.

acid   A substance that tastes sour, neutralizes bases, and turns purple cabbage juice red.

AFIS (Automatic Fingerprint Identification System)   A computerized system that can compare in a matter of minutes a fingerprint to one of 25 million samples stored in its memory.

anatomy   The field of science that studies the structure of living organisms.

anthropology   The field of science that studies humans, especially their physical and cultural characteristics, customs, and social relationships.

arson   The criminal act of burning property such as a building.

ballistics   The field of science that deals with the motion and impact of shot objects, such as bullets and rockets.

base   A substance that tastes bitter, neutralizes acids, and turns purple cabbage juice green.

biology   The field of science that studies the origin, history, and characteristics of plants and animals.

botany   The field of science that studies plants.

caliber   The diameter of a bullet in inches or millimeters.

cartridge   The cylindrical container of a bullet, which holds the gunpowder.

cast   A form made by pouring plaster of paris into a mold.

cheiloscopy   The study of lip prints.

chemistry   The field of science that deals with the makeup and properties of substances and with the reactions that are produced when chemicals are combined.

chromatography   A process by which complex chemicals, such as ink, are separated into the chemicals of which they are made.

chromosome   One of 46 microscopic bodies that are contained in the nucleus of a cell and that carry the genes that convey hereditary characteristics.

clues   Real, measurable, countable observations of a crime and a crime scene.

contact trace theory   The theory, first recognized by Edmond Locard in 1910, that states that a criminal will always take something from the scene of his or her crime and leave something behind.

convict   To find guilty in a court of law.

counterfeit   To make an imitation of something genuine so as to deceive or defraud; something that has been counterfeited.

crime   An act that is against the law.

crime lab   The forensic laboratory where evidence is analyzed.

criminology   The scientific study and investigation of crime and criminals.

deciduous teeth   The first set of human teeth, replaced by permanent teeth beginning at about age six.

decomposition   The natural process of decay of materials.

detective   A special police officer who is responsible for investigating serious crimes.

diatom   A form of microscopic algae that contains a sandlike substance called silica in its cell wall.

DNA (deoxyribonucleic acid)   The chemical compounds that form the basic material in the chromosomes of the cell nucleus. DNA contains the genetic code that is basically the recipe for the human body.

DNA profiling   A forensic test that links cells found at the scene of a crime to the DNA of a suspect.

dusting   A technique by which fingerprints are coated with powder so that they may be lifted and taken to a crime lab for identification.

entomologist   A scientist who studies insects.

evidence   An object that provides proof of a crime, especially in a court of law.

fingerprint   An impression of the friction ridges of the end joint of a person's finger, used to identify the person.

firing pin   The metal part of a gun that strikes the cartridge and ignites the gunpowder.

forensic   Suitable for a court of law.

forensic laboratory   The place where evidence is analyzed, commonly called the crime lab.

forensic science   The field of science that deals with the application of scientific knowledge to legal matters, especially those involved in the investigation of a crime.

forge To copy with the intent to deceive.

forgery The act of falsifying or counterfeiting documents.

friction ridges The tiny, raised lines on the palms of hands and the soles of feet that leave prints.

gel electrophoresis The process by which DNA pieces are separated from one another into bands according to size.

gene The part of a chromosome that causes traits, such as eye color and hair color.

Henry System A system of fingerprint identification that uses numbers to classify the characteristics of a fingerprint as well as the type of finger and hand from which it came.

humus The organic part of soil, consisting of partially decayed plant and animal matter.

hypothesis An educated guess about a problem, such as how a crime was committed and who did it; a possible solution that will be tested by an investigation or experiment.

implicate To reveal, by accident or on purpose, that someone was involved in a crime.

inferences Reasonable conclusions based on evidence.

inorganic From nonliving material.

jigsaw method A method of analyzing glass fragments by putting the pieces of glass back together like a jigsaw puzzle.

lands The area inside a gun barrel that remains after the barrel has been grooved.

latent prints Fingerprints that cannot be clearly seen on an object at a crime scene and therefore must be treated to make them visible.

long-term memory Information that remains in memory and can be recalled for a long time.

microbes Microorganisms, especially bacteria.

microorganisms Small living things, usually microscopic plants and animals.

nucleus The center of a cell, which contains DNA and is important in most cellular functions.

observe To note carefully, using all of one's senses to pay attention to details.

organic From living material.

organism   Any living thing.

pathology   The field of science that studies the causes of death and disease.

pelvic bones   The bones that form the hips.

perjury   Purposely lying while under oath.

permanent teeth   The second and final set of teeth, which replace the deciduous teeth between the ages of about six and eighteen.

physiology   The field of science that studies how organisms function.

poaching   The killing of wildlife either without a license or out of season.

rifling grooves   The long, narrow grooves cut around the interior surface of a gun barrel.

rifling marks   Characteristic marks made on a fired bullet by rifling grooves.

root   The enlarged part of a strand of hair that grows below the surface of the skin.

senses   The ability of the brain and nerves to receive and react to the world around us through sight, hearing, smell, touch, and taste.

short-term memory   Recently stored information that can be recalled for a short period of time.

spore   A small cell produced by simple plants, such as bacteria, algae, mosses, and ferns, that can develop into a new individual.

stakeout   Surveillance of an area.

stature   The height of a person.

surveillance   The practice of watching a suspect.

suspect   Someone who is believed to have committed a crime.

tail   To follow a suspect without the suspect's knowledge.

trace evidence   Small bits of material that can be analyzed and used as evidence in a criminal investigation.

visible prints   Fingerprints that can be clearly seen on an object at a crime scene.

voiceprint   A pattern of wavy lines and whorls produced by a recording of a person's voice and used to identify the person.

zoology   The field of science that studies animals.

Index